Cornish
MURDERS

Other books in this series by John Van der Kiste and Nicola Sly

John Van der Kiste & Nicola Sly
Somerset Murders
West Country Murders

John Van der Kiste
Devon Murders
Surrey Murders
Berkshire Murders

Nicola Sly
Bristol Murders
Dorset Murders
Hampshire Murders
Shropshire Murders
Wiltshire Murders
Worcestershire Murders

First published in the United Kingdom in 2007 by Sutton Publishing

Reprinted in 2009 by
The History Press
The Mill, Brismcombe Port,
Stroud, Gloucestershire, GL5 2QG
www.thehistorypress.co.uk

British Library Cataloguing in Publication Data
A catalogue record for this book is available from the British Library.

ISBN 978-0-7509-4707-7

Typeset in 10.5/13.5pt Sabon.
Typesetting and origination by
Sutton Publishing.
Printed and bound in England.

Cornish
MURDERS

John Van der Kiste & Nicola Sly

The
History
Press

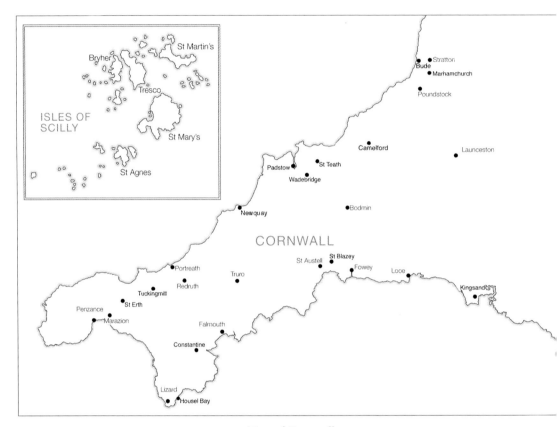

Map of Cornwall.

CONTENTS

FOREWORD

A look at the annals of true crime in the most south-westerly part of mainland Britain reveals a fascinating if chilling tapestry of murder. There are episodes of robbery with violence that resulted in fatalities, domestic disputes which went too far, and unwanted or inconvenient infants quietly disposed of. Some went almost unnoticed outside the local community, while others – particularly the manhunt leading to the arrest of Edward Black for the killing of his wife in 1921, and the frenzied attack by Miles Giffard on his parents thirty years later – resulted in detailed coverage in the national press. A few murders remain unsolved to this day, some led to the perpetrator's suicide, and some resulted in trial and acquittal.

The cases featured in this volume span almost one and a half centuries, from the poisoning of Henry Polgrean and the killing of William Hancock on market day at Helston in 1820, to the murder of recluse William Rowe at his farm near Constantine in 1963, the last but one murder trial which resulted in the guilty men going to the gallows before the death penalty was effectively abolished in the United Kingdom.

In our researches we have relied heavily on the work of previous authors in the field, all of whose relevant works are listed in the bibliography, as well as local and national newspapers, via microfilm and the internet. We would also like to acknowledge the assistance of Jill and Adrian Abbott; Ann Heasman; Angela Sutton-Vane; Wesley Mills; Colin Webb; and the staff at the Cornish Studies Library, Redruth; the Royal Cornwall Museum, Truro; Plymouth City Libraries; Bude Library; and The Heritage and Learning Resource of Devon and Cornwall Constabulary, Okehampton.

Particular thanks are due to Kim and Kate Van der Kiste (John's wife and mother) and Richard Sly and John Higginson (Nicola's husband and father) for their encouragement, advice, reading through the manuscript in draft form, and assistance with the photography. Finally, thanks go to our editors at Sutton Publishing, Simon Fletcher, Matilda Pearce and Michelle Tilling.

1

BREAD, BUTTER
AND ARSENIC

Ludgvan, 1820

Sarah Polgrean (spelled Polgreen in some sources) had a hard life. Born in Gulval near Penzance, her father was killed in an accident in London and, at just four months old, her mother abandoned her to the care of the parish. Uneducated and totally illiterate, she was apprenticed into service at the age of nine, where it appears she was sexually abused by at least one other servant. When her apprenticeship ended, she took to drifting around the country, never settling in one place for too long. At one stage she even located her mother and lived with her for a few months, but found her cold and indifferent. The relationship between them was certainly not the loving one that Sarah craved.

She met and married a soldier who took her to London, but the couple soon realised that they were ill matched and parted by mutual consent. Once again she moved on, eventually arriving back in the county of her birth. In Ludgvan, near Penzance, she met and married Henry Polgrean.

Yet again, the union was an unhappy one. Sarah, it seemed, was somewhat free with her sexual favours and was incapable of remaining faithful to her marriage vows. Not unreasonably, Henry was jealous. The couple had frequent rows during which Sarah, who had grown to hate her husband, was often heard to threaten to poison him.

On Friday 14 July 1820, Henry fell ill. He vomited that evening and, on the following day, a surgeon was called to attend to him. After examining Henry, the surgeon concluded that he had simply eaten something that disagreed with him and recommended that he should be bled. This was done and, afterwards, he felt well enough to eat some bread and butter which Sarah had prepared for him.

Yet soon after eating his meal, Henry's condition worsened, and despite the best efforts of the surgeon he died. After his death, rumours about Sarah abounded until they reached fever pitch. Eventually the local police could ignore the gossip no longer. Eleven days after his burial, his body was exhumed and the contents of his stomach analysed. It was found that he had consumed a lethal quantity of arsenic.

In view of the unhappy state of his marriage, police concentrated their enquiries on his widow and soon discovered that Sarah had recently bought arsenic from a shop in nearby Penzance, claiming it was to be used for killing rats at home.

Since the house had never been known to have a problem with vermin, Sarah was quickly arrested and charged with the wilful murder of her husband.

Her trial opened at Bodmin Assizes on 10 August 1820. Despite Sarah's protestations of her innocence, after hearing the overwhelming evidence against her the jury were quick to find her guilty. The presiding judge passed the mandatory death sentence, instructing that her body should afterwards be given for dissection. At this, a distressed Sarah slumped into a faint and had to be carried from the court to Bodmin Gaol to await her execution.

Once incarcerated, Sarah decided to make a full confession to her part in Henry's death. She admitted to buying arsenic and to mixing it with a portion of butter. On Saturday 16 July, after the surgeon had bled the ailing Henry, she had spread some bread with the poisoned butter and watched as her husband ate it. She attributed her crime to a lack of religious education and to her early seduction by a fellow servant during her time in service. She hoped that her fate would act as a warning to others who were tempted to commit crimes, particularly those of murder and adultery.

On 12 August 1820, at 12.15 p.m., Sarah was carried to the gallows at Bodmin Gaol on a hurdle. She mounted the platform with a brisk, unfaltering step and, before a large crowd of spectators, she enthusiastically joined in with the prayers and the singing of a final hymn. She then appealed to the crowd to take solemn warning from her predicament. Finally, having shaken hands with the executioner and his attendant, she gave the signal that she was ready and was quickly despatched. She was in her mid-thirties at the time of her execution.

THE CONDEMNED CELL, BODMIN GAOL.

2

DEATH ON MARKET DAY

Helston, 1820

On 12 August 1820, farmer William Williams Hancock from the parish of Mullion was returning home after a day spent at Helston market. As he reached Base Corner, with around two miles of his journey still to complete, he was accosted by three men, one of whom grabbed the bridle of his grey horse.

Ignoring the men's demands to stop, Hancock urged his horse onwards and, as he did, it trod on the foot of the man holding the bridle. As Hancock escaped, a shot rang out and several slugs from a musket peppered the unfortunate farmer, causing him to fall from his horse. As soon as he fell, the three men attacked him again, stealing the new hat he had bought at the market and rifling through his pockets. They must have been disappointed to find a haul of just two shillings, since they kicked and beat the man as he lay injured, eventually leaving him for dead on the roadside.

Hancock was found by neighbours and removed to a house about a quarter of a mile away. While he was there, more shots were heard, followed by the frightened screams of a woman. Knowing that armed robbers were at large, nobody ventured outside to check on the source of the noise, but it was later established that there had been another attempted robbery, apparently committed by the same three men.

The next victims, labourer William Jose and his wife, were also returning from Helston market when they were set upon by the same gang of men. Although both were seriously wounded, most of the slugs from the robbers' muskets lodged in a joint of meat carried by Mrs Jose in a basket on her arm. Her screams were sufficiently loud to cause their attackers to flee empty handed. The injured couple managed to reach a nearby house, where they claimed to have recognised their attackers, naming them as John Barnicoat and brothers Thomas and John Thompson.

The following morning, the three suspects were brought before Hancock, who also identified Barnicoat and John Thompson as two of the three men who had robbed him. The farmer stated that Barnicoat had hit him with a long pole after he had been shot. Barnicoat denied this, but Hancock accused him of lying, asking how he could say that when he had stood over him with a pole and threatened to knock his brains out?

William Hancock died from his injuries on the following Thursday, and, as a result of his dying declaration, Barnicoat and the Thompson brothers were arrested. When the dragoons went to apprehend them, Barnicoat was found to be limping. A buried gun was found at the home of the Thompson brothers, as was Mr Hancock's new hat. Finally, a search of the Thompson home yielded a scythe handle, in which were embedded grey hairs, similar to those from the coat of Hancock's horse. Barnicoat protested his innocence, claiming that his foot was hurt when his own horse stepped on it. He swore that he had been at home in bed nursing his injury at the time of the murder. Despite his protestations, the three men were arrested and committed for trial.

The trial opened on 30 March 1821, and Barnicoat was able to produce two witnesses who provided him with an alibi for the night of the murder. However, as might be expected from two independent witnesses who had not collaborated on their respective stories, certain details of their sworn statements differed and the jury chose to disbelieve them. When called upon to plead, Thomas Thompson said, 'Guilty of being with them, but – ' when the judge broke in and told him to plead 'Not guilty'. Because he had not been named in Hancock's deathbed statement, Thomas Thompson was acquitted. John Barnicoat, aged twenty-four and seventeen-year-old John Thompson were both found guilty and sentenced to death by hanging.

Barnicoat continued to protest his innocence to the end. On Monday 2 April 1821, the two men were led to a scaffold that had been erected on the Castle Green, adjacent to Launceston Gaol. Barnicoat approached his fate stoically, while Thompson had to be given a chair to sit on, since he trembled so much on reaching the platform. The prison chaplain stepped forward and asked Barnicoat if he still maintained that he was innocent. Barnicoat did, turning to Thompson beside him and appealing to him to tell the truth.

Thompson promptly confirmed Barnicoat's story, stating that the three men involved had been himself, his brother William and a farmer named Thomas Dawe. According to Thompson, Dawe had fired the shots at both Hancock and Mr and Mrs Jose and he himself had beaten Hancock with a pole, which he described as a pike handle. Barnicoat and Thompson's protests were in vain. After a final few moments spent in prayer with the chaplain, both were hung before a large crowd of spectators.

So who was responsible for the death of William Hancock and the serious injuries to Mr Jose and his wife?

Given the confession by John Thompson in his final moments, his appears to be the only constant name put forward as a guilty party. While his brother William was never charged with the murder, anecdotal evidence suggests that witnesses reported seeing Dawe's dog at the scene of the crimes and so assumed that the dog's master was also present. However, there are several other theories as to the identities of the murderers.

The first theory is that the wrong Barnicoat was hanged. John Barnicoat was the son of a relatively well-to-do family and therefore had no motive to commit robbery. However, there was, at the time, another man named Barnicoat in the area, an itinerant farm labourer from Tregony, who moved from farm to farm helping with the harvests.

It was reported in *The Times* that it was this gentleman, known only as J.E. Barnicoat, who had murdered Hancock in the course of committing highway robbery. J.E. Barnicoat allegedly fled hurriedly to Australia to escape justice, but suffered from terrible pangs of conscience over the hanging of his namesake. It is said that when he died in Australia, he bequeathed his estate to the family of John Barnicoat, to try to make amends for the wrong done to them. Was it possible that both Mr and Mrs Jose and William Hancock all identified the wrong Barnicoat as their assailant?

A second theory revolves around another local farmer from Lemana in Cury, near Helston. John Dale apparently married a Miss Thompson, believed to be a relative of the Thompson brothers. After being severely kicked by a horse, Dale allegedly made a deathbed confession to the murder, stating that it was him who should have been hanged in place of Barnicoat. Dale apparently died in 1833, aged ninety years. If he was guilty of the crime, he would have been in his late seventies when it was committed, hardly an age when previously respectable farmers turn suddenly to a criminal lifestyle.

Almost two centuries later, the mystery of the murder of William Hancock and the subsequent vicious attack on Mr and Mrs Jose seems unlikely to be satisfactorily solved. The most plausible solution seems to be that confessed by Thompson on the scaffold – that he and his brother, William, accompanied by Thomas Dawe, were guilty of the crimes. Yet, while a number of possible scenarios can be argued, one fact seems to be beyond doubt. That is that John Barnicoat, an innocent man, paid the ultimate price for a crime he did not commit.

3

'SHOULD YOU LIKE TO GO TO HEAVEN, DEAR?'

Redruth, 1824

'Murder – Extraordinary Fanaticism', thundered a headline in *The Times* on 6 April 1824. The subject of this sad story was no 'extraordinary fanatic', but an apparently innocent gentle young girl of nineteen convinced she was acting from the best of motives, but whose behaviour was to plunge the family into tragedy.

Amy (sometimes known as Emma) George lived in Redruth with her family and worked in the local tin mine. Sometime around January 1824 she began to attend Methodist, Methodist Revival and class meetings in the town. Whether she had shown any signs of mental instability in her earlier years is not recorded. However the unbounded enthusiasm – not to say fanaticism – of the preachers who led these meetings, and of those others who attended with her, must have had an extremely unsettling effect on the impressionable girl's mind.

One night at about 10.30 p.m., her mother fetched her home from a meeting. Amy had been there for over eight hours, and when Mrs George arrived she found the chapel extremely crowded. That would not in itself have been sufficient cause for concern. What did alarm her was Amy's peculiar behaviour. When she caught sight of her mother, the girl lifted up her arms 'as if she was going to fly to the top of the room', and called on her mother and father to pray to the Lord to help them, as 'they could not see what danger they were in'. She got Amy out of the meeting as quickly as she could, but she had lost her cloak, bonnet, handkerchief and pattens (wooden-soled shoes), 'and was extremely disordered in her dress'. When Mrs George questioned her about it, the girl said she had been moving from one part of the meeting to another, had dropped her clothes and they must have got trodden underfoot. The girl's conduct at home, she was certain, was quite different after that night to what it had normally been before.

After another meeting, Amy came home praying in what her mother thought 'a horrible manner' – in other words, quite excitable, her treatment bordering on mental derangement – for the conversion of her parents. It was not long before Mrs George feared that her daughter would start behaving violently. On the evening of 1 March Amy returned home from another meeting, sat by the fire, and said sadly, 'Mother, I am going out of my mind.' Her mother tried to reassure her, whereupon she calmed down and went to bed.

On the following night Amy said she felt better, but still seemed unusually dispirited. Unknown to anyone else, she was beginning to descend into an ugly spiral from which there would be no escape. On the evening of 3 March, she told her mother quite matter-of-factly that she was tempted to murder her. Trying hard to humour her, Mrs George said she was most surprised, but Amy was not to be dissuaded and assured her she meant it. 'I do', she repeated. After that she went to another Revival meeting, and her mother took advantage of her absence to hide any knives in the interests of self-preservation.

She was not the only one to be disturbed by the state of Amy's mind. A family friend, Mrs Osborne, had seen her the previous month. Amy told her she had been unwell, 'and that her illness was in her head; it appeared to her, she said, as if the top part of her head was heaving off', and she said that her brains felt as if they had been 'turned'. Amy, Mrs Osborne thought, was in rather a wild state, 'and her eyes were rolling in her head in a very vicious manner.' Mrs Osborne told her she should not give way to such thoughts, and taking a copy of the Bible, read her a few words from the book of Genesis. This seemed to pacify her for a while.

John Cocking, a constable of Redruth, was also witness to Amy's peculiar state of mind that week. She had told him of her intention to commit a murder, probably that of her mother, but she tried to put the idea totally out of her mind, to the extent of praying to God to take the temptation away from her. Any recovery proved only temporary, for on the morning of 4 March, while she was working at the mine, the idea came back to her even more strongly than before. Around midday she went to get her dinner from the boiling-house. While there she recollected having seen a little boy, a stranger to her, standing by the engine house, near the mouth of a pit, and regretted not having taken the opportunity to seize him and throw him down the shaft. Such an unpleasant idea must have been preying on her mind throughout the afternoon, for when she returned home that evening, she noticed two children playing near another mineshaft alongside the road. She said to herself that she would throw one of them down. As she stood and watched them in their game, they came running in her direction, but she could not bring herself to do so. Walking home she noticed more children, and still she had an overpowering urge to throw one of them down, but so many people were walking past that she was denied the opportunity.

After waiting for some time to see if there was a chance of grabbing one without being noticed, she gave up, went home and found her mother was going to a meeting. Mrs George told her that her supper was ready and that her little brother Benny, aged six, would be staying in with her.

In her own words, Amy 'felt glad I had the opportunity of doing the thing I long wished for – that I was going to be left alone with my little brother, and that my mother was going to be out of the way, so that I should be able to do the deed.' She took her supper and sat at the end of the table, offered Benny some, and asked him, 'Should you like to go to heaven, dear?' 'Yes, when I die,' he answered.

She got up, went to a washing line hanging across the room, took down a black silk handkerchief and proceeded to tie it round his neck. When she asked him if it was too tight, he smiled and assured her it was not. She left the handkerchief round his neck and said, 'Go for a drop of water for me, dear.' Her intention had been for him to go and fetch a pail, and while his back was turned, to take him up and hang him from a crook behind the door. He was quicker than she had expected him to be, and when he brought the water back she took it from him, drank a little and put the cup on the table. Then she picked Benny up with one arm, and with the other put the handkerchief over the crook, looked him full in the face as she suspended him – and left the room.

A little later she went to visit her neighbours; Francis Hodge, his wife and their two children. After enquiring as to their health, Amy remarked, 'I wish I could go to heaven.' Francis told her in that case she would have to 'make a good preparation to try to get there, better than you have lately.' Noticing the troubled look on her face, he asked her what the matter was. 'Oh! What shall I do, what shall I do?' she asked, wringing her hands. 'What have you done?' he asked. Had she fallen out with anybody? She shook her head, clasped her hands firmly and confessed that she had hanged her little brother Benny, and put him on a crook behind the door.

Francis leapt to his feet and ran towards her house. On his way he saw a friend, Mr Gribble, who was already aware of what had happened. They went to rescue Benny George, took hold of his feet and cut the handkerchief, but as his body fell to the floor they could see they were too late. Returning to the room where Amy was sitting, they asked her what she had done. 'I have hanged my little brother, and I am willing to die for it,' she told them.

That evening Samuel Gribble had been visiting his father, who lived in one of the tenements in the same house as the Georges. While he was there, he heard Mrs Hodge screaming. He went and took the candle from her hand, walked into Amy's room and saw the little boy hanging from a crook in the beam. Francis Hodge and the elder Mr Gribble cut him down, while Samuel asked Amy what she had done. She had hanged her brother, she said, as she wanted to send him to heaven, and she wanted to cut her own throat so she could join him there. She seemed to be 'in a deranged state of mind', and he tried to restrain her from going to find a knife there and then. Yet she remained adamant that she was going to cut her throat, so Samuel remained with her until one or two women from the family came into the room and he was able to leave her in their care.

Amy was sent for trial at Launceston on 1 April on a charge of murdering her brother. On being placed at the bar, it was reported she 'appeared in the deepest affliction, which operated so powerfully on her feelings, that a long time elapsed before her senses reminded her of the awful investigation that was about to take place.'

The basic facts of the case were beyond doubt. What the jury had to decide was whether the prisoner was a responsible agent at the time, capable of telling right from wrong. For the prosecution, Mr Tancred said that if the jury believed 'that her judgment was so defective as not to be able to make that distinction, then the retributive claims of the public for the act she had committed were to be laid aside and forgotten'. On the other hand, if they should decide that when she committed the fatal act, 'she was under the influence of a melancholy delusion, but which delusion she was not sufficiently strong to deprive her of reason, they would not, from feelings of compassion, withhold that protection to themselves and society which was entrusted as their care to preserve.'

Francis Hodge, Samuel Gribble and John Cocking were among those called as witnesses to recount the facts of the case. How responsible her attendance at the Methodist Revival meetings had been was discussed at length. Constable Cocking declared that their conduct was 'wild and extravagant, and altogether out of the mild and decent course of addressing the Almighty, usually observed in places of worship.' Whereas most people would not be adversely affected by attending, there was the potential to do considerable harm in the case of young people with weak minds. If Amy George had been unstable or weak-minded, her attendance at what Cocking called a meeting of 'screeching for mercy' could have done considerable harm to her mental condition.

Throughout the trial, Amy herself seemed unable to answer or say anything in her defence, and sat there with an apparent lack of interest in what was going on around her. After evidence had been given in court she fainted and had to be taken outside for fresh air. As she came round, she struggled so violently that it took about six men to lead her away. Once they were in the street, she proceeded to shout and scream loudly for about quarter of an hour, before she calmed down and the hearing could be resumed.

In his summing up, Mr Justice Burrough said there was no disputing that the young woman at the bar was the cause of her brother's death. Did the jury consider that when she committed the murder she was in a state of mind capable of distinguishing between right and wrong? If it was their opinion 'that she did it in a moment when the imbecility of her mind was so great that she could not make that distinction, then the offence did not amount to wilful murder'. The evidence suggested that 'it was almost impossible to conceive that the prisoner could be otherwise than insane when she determined on the murder of her own brother, as the means of getting to heaven. The Almighty had expressly declared that murder and suicide were two of the highest crimes that called for his vengeance; but such was the delusion this young woman had laboured under, that she first murdered her brother, and then contemplated self-destruction, conceiving that by committing these high offences she should be securing a way to heaven.'

The religious meetings she had been attending had evidently played a large part. While the judge admitted he knew nothing of the sect spoken of in court, and while the last thing he wanted to do was to be seen as wishing to restrain anybody from following the religious customs most comfortable to their conscience, he could not but take account of the fact that 'the doctrines and mode of worship which inculcated the pernicious principles this young woman had acted upon, were injurious to society, and ought to be suppressed.' Her mind was under the impression that 'religious excitations' had inspired her to commit a murder before she could get to heaven.

At first she had decided that her mother, 'as the object who was to be devoted to her frenzy', would have to die. Next she was going to choose one or other of the children in the area whom she had never seen before, but finally her brother was going to have to pay the price; 'she murdered him in the same absence of malice as she would have done any other individual'. If members of the jury were of the opinion that the child lost his life while she was in a state of insanity, they had to return a verdict of not guilty on those grounds, and she would be protected by the full force of law 'till she was found to be sufficiently restored to her reason to be returned to her friends'.

There was only one possible verdict, and the jury accordingly found her not guilty. The court ordered her to be retained in custody, while assuring her family and friends 'she would not be kept long from them'.

4

FIZZY MAGGY

Gwennap, 1836

The mining parish of Gwennap, lying to the south-east of Redruth, has strong historical links with the Methodist faith in Cornwall. During the eighteenth century John Wesley preached there on eighteen occasions, targeting its frequently impoverished parishioners with the message that, while earthly rewards may be few, there was a reward in heaven for those who accepted the Lord. According to the census of 1831 the population was a mere 8,539, rising to 10,794 persons over the following ten years.

One of its inhabitants, Philip Manuel, was by all accounts a madman in every sense of the word. Thomas Bray, a local police constable, knew him well and was convinced that he and his entire family – father, mother, brother and sister – were quite mad. Grown men of the area declared they were too afraid to pass his house at Carnmarth because of his strange behaviour. He was frequently the object of taunting and tormenting from local children, who had been heard to call him 'Fizzy Maggy'.

A married man with several children, he was aged sixty-one at the time he committed the deed that was to make him notorious. Because of his violent behaviour, a court order had temporarily removed the children from his custody and they were living at a different address nearby with their mother. This separation had come about when he allegedly tried to smother his son, a boy of whom he was said to be 'exceedingly fond'. He denied 'stifling' the boy but, when called upon to investigate the incident, Constable Bray unearthed a large cache of weapons beneath Manuel's bed. Manuel explained to the officer that he needed to keep these weapons to hand since, he insisted, 'people were going to rob him'.

His extreme fear of falling victim to theft surfaced again early in 1836. He approached several people in the neighbourhood in a highly anguished state, foaming at the mouth, crying noisily and complaining that 'people were going to rob and murder him'.

On 19 February his daughters, Caroline and Christian, visited him at home. It was apparent that he was in no mood to receive visitors, as he refused to let the girls into the house. When they appeared, he shouted at them to leave. They cheekily called him a rude name, at which he immediately grabbed his gun and gave chase. Thoroughly frightened, they ran to a neighbour, Martha Matthews, but she turned them away, refusing to take sides in a family argument. Manuel then discharged his gun, firing at Caroline from a distance of about 10ft. A shot hit her in the head and she died from her injuries shortly afterwards.

At Manuel's trial at the Cornwall Assizes, held in Launceston in March 1836, numerous people testified to his peculiarities of behaviour. These included his surviving daughter, Christian, who stated that the family believed her father to be insane in the light of his earlier attempted murder of her brother. The jury found Manuel guilty of the cold-blooded murder of his daughter but stated that, at the time of the killing, they believed the defendant to be of unsound mind, bordering on insanity. He was sentenced to life imprisonment.

5

'COME. I SUPPOSE SHE HAS FOUND THE LORD NOW'

Trevarth, 1839

Jesse Lean lived in the small village of Trevarth, where he worked in the mines and ran a small farm. He and his wife, Loveday, were well respected in the area and, having lived rather frugally and saved a good proportion of Jesse's earnings over the years, were financially comfortable as they approached their old age. Indeed, it was rumoured that Jesse kept substantial sums of money at home.

On Wednesday 6 February 1839, Jesse rose early as usual, had his breakfast and then went out to his barn to check on the horses. While there he thought he heard someone moving about. He called out but received no answer, so he went to the lane outside the barn to see if he could see anybody. There he met a neighbour, Stephen Jeffrey, who asked who he had been calling. Lean asked Jeffrey if he had seen anyone and Jeffrey replied that he had seen a man or boy – had he done any harm? Lean told him that the mysterious stranger had simply rattled the door latch and run away.

The horses attended to, Lean went back into the house to complete his morning chores. Having lit the fire, he then walked through the darkness to the mine, greeting his fellow workers before starting his grading job. Shortly afterwards, he was approached by another mine worker, John Oxford, who told him that a messenger had arrived on horseback bearing the news that Loveday Lean was unwell and that Jesse was needed urgently at home.

Samuel Trengrove, a near neighbour of the Lean family, was employed by Jesse to work his horses. Trengrove had reported for work as normal, shortly after Jesse had left for the mine, to find the back door of the house open. As he approached, he had heard Loveday calling out for help. He entered the house to find her bloody and beaten, begging him to fetch his mother because she was dying. Samuel had first summoned his mother, Grace, to attend to their neighbour, before riding as fast as he could to the mine to inform Jesse of his wife's condition.

Jesse came to the surface, where he found Trengrove waiting for him. 'Is she dead or alive?' Lean asked Samuel, to be reassured that, when Samuel had left, Loveday was alive and safe in the care of his mother.

Lean hastened home to find Loveday blood-soaked but still conscious, with severe head injuries. He held his wife and asked her what had happened, to which she replied that a man in a brown coat had forced his way into her bedroom and 'clopped' her over the head. Several neighbours who were present at the time heard her say this and she later repeated her account to the doctor who was summoned to attend her injuries.

Dr George Michell did little more than clean and bandage Loveday's wounds before returning home. Throughout the day, Loveday made little improvement and, the same evening, Jesse Lean visited Dr Michell in search of medicine for his wife. Sadly, his visit proved pointless as she died later that night.

An autopsy later revealed that Loveday Lean had been stabbed three times in the face and once in her ear. Her death was as a result of ruptured blood vessels in the brain arising from the stab wounds.

As was often the case when a wife was murdered, Jesse Lean was the most obvious suspect, particularly since it was known that he and Loveday had quarrelled at times. A search of the house revealed that nothing had been stolen in the course of the murder, which seemed initially to rule out robbery as the motive. However Jesse was exonerated when other witnesses confirmed his movements and the police were forced to cast their net wider in an effort to find Loveday's killer. Lean told police that on the previous night his wife and a neighbour, Jane Bray, had been taking tea at his home. Someone had opened the door to the cottage, but had neither called out nor entered the house.

Stephen Jeffrey told them about the man he had seen on the morning of the murder, who, it seemed, had been prowling round the barn and was disturbed when Lean went to check on his horses. The man had run past him on Trevarth Lane and eventually attempted to open Jeffrey's cottage door without success. Bearing in mind how dark it was at that time of the morning, Jeffrey was only able to give the scantiest of descriptions of the prowler, whom he described as 'a brave, hardy youngster'.

Another miner, William Nicholls, had been walking past the Lean's house a little later in the morning and heard a commotion from inside which he described as a woman moaning and crying to the Lord. He had waited outside the house for a few minutes, listening to the frightful noise, before being approached by Betsy Martin, another neighbour. He had told Betsy that since she was a Methodist she should go in and see what she could do, but Betsy was too afraid to enter the house. As the two stood discussing whether or not they should investigate further, they had heard a thump from the bedroom, which Nicholls attributed to someone either jumping out of bed or jumping up from their knees. 'Come. I suppose she has found the Lord now,' he commented to Betsy and the two moved on, with Nicholls gallantly pushing Martin's wheelbarrow for her.

Eventually police apprehended a local youth, a miner named William White, aged about fifteen or sixteen. He was well known in the village as an idle layabout, and was described as having a 'forbidding, scampish appearance'. Asked to account for his whereabouts on the day of the murder, White explained that he had previously been employed at Poldory mine, but had lost his job. He had then made enquiries at Consols mine, but was unsuccessful in finding any further work, so he had spent most of the day hanging around aimlessly at the blacksmith's shop, before lying down in William Martin's barn and falling asleep. There he stayed until 5 a.m. the following day.

At the coroner's inquest into the death of Loveday Lean, numerous witnesses came forward to give evidence. Among them was Stephen Jeffrey, who stated that he did not think that White resembled the man he had seen running in the lane on the morning of the murders, specifically because the coat the stranger had been wearing was longer than that worn by White.

William Nicholls stated that, shortly before he had heard the moaning and crying coming from the Leans' cottage, he had in fact seen another man on the lane between there and the house belonging to the Lean's neighbours, the Martin family. Nicholls named the man he had seen as a local youth, Thomas Pope. However John Paul, the village blacksmith, denied that William White was at his shop at any time during the day of the murder, effectively destroying White's alibi.

The inquest was able to establish that practically every word of White's statement was a lie. What it was not possible to do was to place White at the murder scene or to find any conclusive evidence that he had been involved in any way. As a result the jury, having deliberated for a short time, gave a verdict of 'Wilful murder against some person or persons to the jurors unknown.' It was believed that robbery may have been the motive for the vicious attack on the elderly lady and that the perpetrator may have been disturbed in the course of the robbery and fled empty handed.

After the coroner's Inquest, a reward was offered by the parish for the discovery of the murderer of Loveday Lean, and it was anticipated that the government would increase the amount offered (£50) in due course. Soon afterwards a man named Cock made a full confession to the murder and was held in police custody for a week. He later retracted his confession and, in the absence of any evidence against him, was released without charge. Police then turned their attention back to Jesse Lean but once again found insufficient evidence to charge him with the murder of his wife.

Records show that a Jesse Lean of Redruth died during the second quarter of 1840, the year after the murder. It is not absolutely certain whether or not the deceased was the same man, but investigations into the murder subsequently seemed to peter out, suggesting that the police at the time still considered Jesse Lean as their main suspect. Officially the identity of the killer of Loveday Lean remains unknown.

6

'DO, WILLY, GO AND CONFESS'

Wadebridge, 1840

On 8 February 1840, the merchant ship *Orient* was sailing en route from Manila to Cadiz. As it drew near St Helena its captain, Edmund Norway, was writing a letter to his brother Nevell, a well-known and highly-respected local timber and general trader, aged thirty-nine, who lived in Cornwall. Having finished his letter, Norway recorded in the ship's log that he retired to bed at about 10.45 p.m. His sleep that night was anything but peaceful, being disturbed by what he later described as a 'dreadful dream' in which he 'saw' his brother riding along the road from St Columb to Wadebridge. To his horror he dreamed that Nevell was accosted by two men, one of whom grabbed the bridle of the horse he was riding. A pistol was fired twice, but Captain Norway heard no sound. Then he saw one of the men strike his brother, causing him to fall from his horse. Nevell was severely beaten, dragged by the shoulders across the road and left for dead in a ditch.

When called to watch at 4 a.m., Captain Norway recounted his nightmare to his second officer, Henry Wren, remarking that in the dream a house which he knew to be on the right-hand side of the road had inexplicably moved to the left-hand side. Although Wren made light of the dream, joking about the superstitions of Cornishmen, Captain Norway was sufficiently disturbed by it to record the details in his ship's log.

Back in Cornwall, on 7 February, there had been a rare incidence of highway robbery. The victim, a miller named Derry, had enjoyed a prosperous day at Wadebridge market and had stopped at a public house on his way home to spend some of his profits. As he enjoyed a few drinks, he failed to notice that he was being closely but surreptitiously watched and, on leaving the pub, he had ridden only a short way when three men jumped out of the hedge and knocked him off his horse. Somewhat befuddled by the effects of his celebratory drinks, Mr Derry was unable to offer much resistance as the men rifled through his pockets, making off with approximately £75.

On the following day Nevell Norway set off to ride home from Bodmin to Wadebridge. It was a moonlit night and, for the first part of his journey home, Nevell was accompanied by a farming acquaintance, Abraham Hambly. The latter was aware of the robbery of Mr Derry and, as a precaution, he had armed himself with two pistols, vowing to 'let daylight into the person of any man who might venture to attack him'. They parted company at Mount Charles gate, leaving Nevell to complete his travels alone. His road was isolated, but even at that late hour, quite well travelled.

He would have passed the house at Clapper, belonging to Mr Pollard. Just before Norway rode by, Pollard received a visitor, a preacher named Mr Harley. Seeing a man waiting outside the house, Harley had assumed that he was a manservant and had handed him his horse. When the mistake was discovered, Pollard and Harley went outside to investigate, finding the horse safely tethered to a fence and the mysterious stranger nowhere to be seen.

Later that night, John Hick and Christopher Bowen were riding the same route. On reaching Sladesbridge, just outside Wadebridge, they were hailed by a man shouting, 'Stop! The horse is gone on before.' Assuming that the man was tipsy, the two riders hurried on their way, but before long they spotted a loose horse in front of them, which galloped away as they approached it. A passer-by told them that he too had seen the horse and it bore a strong resemblance to Mr Norway's grey mare. Feeling uneasy, the two men went to Nevell Norway's house. Not wishing to alarm Nevell's wife, they instead approached his waggoner, Thomas Gregory, told him about the loose horse and asked if his master was at home. Gregory checked the stables and found that the horse had returned home riderless, bearing a heavily bloodstained saddle.

Hick and Bowen rode off in search of a surgeon, while Gregory and another servant, Edward Cavell, set out to retrace Norway's route home in search of the missing man. It did not take them long to find him. About two miles away, at North Hill, they noticed some scuff marks on the road, as if something had been dragged across it. Lifting their lantern, they could just make out a bulky shape lying in a ditch at the roadside. It was Nevell Norway, who lay seemingly lifeless on his back in the water, his feet pointing towards the road.

Hoisting the body onto the horse, they made haste back towards Wadebridge, meeting Hick and Bowen on their way. The two men had roused surgeon Mr Trehane Tickle from his bed, and it was he who examined the body at Norway's home, pronouncing him dead. He determined that the victim had received several blows to the head and face from a blunt instrument, causing severe injuries. It was noted that one wound on the chin was darkened, as if contaminated by gunpowder. There were severe cuts to the insides of his lips and he had a broken nose and a particularly deep wound on one eyebrow, beneath which the bone was fractured. The surgeon also found numerous skull fractures which, he determined, would probably have killed him instantly.

When the servant, Edward Cavell, searched his master's clothes, he found his wallet containing £25 in notes, watch and penknife, but noticed that an ivory writing tablet that Norway normally carried was missing, as were his purse and keys. Returning to the place where the body had been found Cavell and Gregory, accompanied by William Norway, a brother of the deceased, found evidence of a struggle having taken place. There were numerous bloodstains at the scene, along with two distinct sets of footprints from what looked like hob-nailed boots and the marks of a bare hand being drawn across the ground. They also found the broken hammer of a gun or pistol and, at a distance of 16ft from the first

The site where Nevell Norway was murdered. (By kind permission of *West Briton*)

bloodstains, a button from Norway's coat, broken into three pieces. His hat lay in a nearby field. In the same field, they spotted a loose dog, which they described as dark bodied, white-faced and 'high on its legs'.

Over the next few days, the same dog was frequently seen at the murder site and, in the belief that its owner might be in some way connected with the murder, several attempts were made to catch it. The dog evaded capture for some time and, even when it was finally trapped, police were unable to establish who the owner was. It was rumoured by local gossips – falsely, as it happened – that the dog had led police to the bloodstained clothes of the murderer, buried in a field close by.

The death was reported to coroner Joseph Hamley the following morning, and he immediately travelled from Bodmin to hold an inquest at the Ship Inn, Wadebridge, that afternoon. Having listened to all the evidence, he requested that members of the public should leave the hearing and recommended that magistrates should investigate the matter further.

The magistrates did not have an easy task. Nevell had been a popular and well-respected businessman in the town, and on the day of his funeral every shop in the town closed for the day. Over 3,000 people took part in the funeral procession, including many of the town dignitaries. Several funds were set up, partly to assist Norway's widow and also to cover the expenses of investigating the crime. Some of this money was put forward as a reward for the apprehension of the murderer and an offer of £100, a small fortune in those days, brought forth a mass of information, almost more than the police could cope with. People were so keen to help with the murder enquiries (and perhaps to get their hands on the reward) that the daily meeting of magistrates in the Molesworth Arms public house quickly descended into chaos. The police were stretched to follow all the leads that came flooding in and, in sorting the wheat from the chaff, wasted a great deal of precious time investigating completely innocent people. They were soon forced to call in two police officers from London to assist in their enquiries.

One man who did provide a useful lead was shoemaker John Harris, who had travelled the same route as Nevell Norway and had noticed two men loitering at the place where the murder was later committed. His description of the two men, particularly of their being 'of short stature', led police to question James Lightfoot, a labourer and petty criminal from the small hamlet of Burlawn, just outside Wadebridge. When twenty-three-year-old James was arrested on suspicion of murder, the nervous reaction of his brother William, aged thirty-six, aroused police suspicions and he too was arrested and taken before the magistrates. Panic-stricken, William sang like a canary, believing that by betraying his brother, he could not only save himself but also claim the £100 reward.

The Lightfoot brothers were sons of the sexton of St Breock near Wadebridge, and had a reputation for being layabouts and ne'er-do-wells, opting for an easy life of crime over an honest day's work. Their criminal exploits included stealing poultry, poaching and housebreaking, in both Cornwall and Devon. Nevell Norway and his family had always treated the Lightfoots with kindness, offering them employment and even helping them financially in times of need. Yet, despite this generosity, neither brother seemed at all perturbed at being brought before the magistrates nor showed any sign of remorse. Both appeared more interested in searching the crowds for familiar faces than in the legal proceedings.

Several witnesses were called to give evidence. One, Richard Caddy, testified that he had been at William's house on the night of the murder and that William had arrived home late, his trousers soaked to the knees. To explain his wet clothes, William claimed he had fallen into a well.

Richard and Elizabeth Ayres, and Elizabeth's mother Betty Bray, were neighbours of James. They told of retiring to bed on the night of the murder, and then being woken in the early hours of the morning by a commotion from the house next door. James' wife was crying noisily while James beseeched her loudly to 'Lie still, damn thee, or folks will hear you.' Her response was that she would not lie still and could not care who heard her.

Richard Caddy had visited James' house on the morning after the murder. There he had seen a distinctive pistol, heavily decorated with brass work. He noticed that the lock and stock were missing but could not draw any further information from James, who simply mumbled about shooting a cat and damaging a screw.

It seemed that the cat story might have been concocted in advance by the two brothers to explain away any bloodstains. Labourer William Verdoe heard about the cat from William Lightfoot who, on the day after his brother James was arrested, turned up for work unusually early and explained that James was 'taken up'. Lightfoot told Verdoe that his brother had shot the animal on the previous Wednesday, bloodying the pistol. He blamed Betty Bray and her family for the trouble his brother was in, saying that if it had not been for them hearing James

James Lightfoot's cottage, St Breock.
(By kind permission of *West Briton*)

coming home so late nobody would have been any the wiser. Although a shot cat was subsequently found in James' garden, Constable William Bray was later able to prove that the pistol stock had been intact and attached to the murder weapon when the animal was despatched.

On 13 February PC Bray conducted a thorough search of James Lightfoot's cottage without finding anything of note. His companion, Constable Joseph Carveth, asked Lightfoot about the pistol and he too was told the story of the cat. Although reluctant to answer any questions about the pistol, the constables persisted and eventually James retrieved the barrel from a ceiling beam and handed it over. The barrel of the pistol contained powder, and, on closer examination, Bray found that it appeared to have been separated very recently from the stock.

A further search of James Lightfoot's house on the following day revealed a paper screw of gunpowder in the pocket of a waistcoat belonging to James and two concealed powder flasks, one empty and one containing powder. In an upstairs room, the police also found the barrel of another gun, while numerous slugs were discovered hidden at various locations around the house. Meanwhile a local farmer had discovered a bundle of papers and a bunch of keys in a furze bush, in a field near where the murder was committed. The keys were found to fit Nevell Norway's house and Norway's brother identified the papers as being accounts, some in his brother's handwriting, some written by his clerk.

Grace Verdoe, William's mother, had visited Burlawn and witnessed the ongoing search for the missing pistol lock. She appealed to William Lightfoot's better nature, saying, 'If you are free, Jemmy [James] is free; if he is guilty, you are guilty. Do, Willy, go and confess.' Her pleas fell on deaf ears. Even when she took him to one side and begged him to tell her about the pistol, he continued to pretend that he did not know what she was talking about. At this, Grace became exasperated. 'You know what you have done,' she told William. 'If you don't confess, I shall tell what you have told my son. If I were you, I would confess, and probably you may have the reward. But if it do go bad with you, perhaps your children will have it.' And with that, she went straight to the house of the local constable, telling his wife to pass on the message that William should also be 'taken up' for his part in the murder.

Both men were escorted to Bodmin Gaol and, on the journey from Wadebridge to Bodmin, each brother was keen to implicate the other. Their journey was broken by a stop at the murder site, where the brothers were persuaded to point out where they had concealed Nevell Norway's keys, personal papers and purse. When shoemaker Richard Harry removed a dresser in settlement of a debt owed to him by James Lightfoot, the missing ivory notebook was found beneath the dresser.

Both men made their confessions before the magistrates. William maintained that his brother had knocked Mr Norway from his horse and beaten him, having first shot at him twice with a pistol, which failed to fire. James's confession accused William of beating Norway with a stick, following the misfiring of the gun, although he admitted to striking the victim several times himself with the butt end of the pistol and assisting his brother in dragging the body to the roadside ditch. In due course they were committed to the assizes for trial.

Shortly before proceedings opened on 20 March 1840, a labourer gathering sticks near the murder site made a significant find. He pulled a stout stick from the hedgerow, which was about fifteen inches long and had a large oval knob on one end measuring about four by three inches. The other end had been whittled with a knife, roughened as if to prevent it being snatched from the hand of an attacker. Despite lying abandoned for some weeks, partially covered in mud and washed by the rain, it still appeared to bear significant traces of blood. The labourer promptly took the stick to magistrates in Wadebridge, where they took steps to try and establish a connection between the weapon and the Lightfoot brothers.

The trial in Bodmin was besieged by crowds of people all hoping to watch the proceedings, many having arrived at the court as early as 6 a.m. The javelin men, whose job it was to escort the judge, had to belabour the spectators with

Above left: *William Lightfoot*. Above right: *James Lightfoot*. (By kind permission of *West Briton*)

their javelins in order to clear a path. Charged with the wilful murder of Nevell Norway in the parish of Egloshayle by beating him over the head and inflicting mortal wounds, both men impassively pleaded 'Not Guilty'.

The prisoners were not legally represented in court, although they were allowed to question the witnesses themselves. They made the most of this opportunity by contradicting as much of the evidence against them as they possibly could. William Verdoe was accused of lying, as was another witness, William Roche, who testified that he was at Bodmin market on the afternoon of the murder and had observed William Lightfoot watching Nevell Norway as he took out his purse to make a payment. London policeman Charles Jackson introduced evidence he had obtained from James during the journey from Wadebridge to Bodmin, to the obvious displeasure of the judge who maintained that he had no right to question the prisoner when he had been committed to appear before magistrates.

The evidence presented at the trial was much the same as that which had been heard by the magistrates. Among the witnesses who testified was Thomas Dungey, a turnkey at Bodmin Gaol, where the brothers had been held in custody pending the trial. According to Dungey, William had been troubled by a guilty conscience on first arriving at the gaol and had wished to unburden himself. He had then confessed his part in the murder to Dungey, stating that it was he who had grabbed the bridle and that he had hit Norway with a stick after James' pistol had misfired. He still maintained that James had struck the fatal blow, he believed with the pistol.

Dungey had left William at that stage and gone to the cell where James was confined. Apparently James had greeted him with a smile, which angered Dungey who exclaimed, 'Good God! How can you smile knowing this dreadful thing hanging over your head?' The gaoler then proceeded to question James about his part in the murder. The judge, Mr Justice Coltman, interrupted to ask if the prisoner had been cautioned at this stage, to which Dungey replied that he had not. At this point, the judge put an end to Dungey's testimony against James, the evidence having been obtained in such an 'objectionable' way.

Once all the evidence had been presented to the court, the judge spoke to each prisoner in turn. First he turned to William, saying; 'If you have any account of this matter to give, you may tell your story or you may say whatever you wish about it.' All William had to say was; 'I never murdered Mr Norway.' Offered the same opportunity to speak, his brother James said only 'I never murdered the man.'

Next, both prisoners were asked if there were any witnesses that they wished to be called. James Lightfoot declined to call any, but William asked for four – two miners named Wills, John Rouncevell and Mary Carveth. William proposed that since all four had seen him leave his home on the day of the murder at about 3 p.m. and, since he lived about six miles from Bodmin, their testimony would cast doubt on the evidence of William Roche who had testified that he had seen Lightfoot observing Norway in Bodmin an hour later. The miners did not appear, but both Rouncevell and Carveth were called. Both seemed vague about the actual time when William Lightfoot had been seen leaving Bodmin. Rouncevell agreed that it was at 'about' 3 p.m., but could not be certain to within half an hour or so. Carveth also testified that William had left at about that hour, but had told the time by her clock, which she admitted was fast.

In summing up the evidence for the jury, Mr Justice Coltman was fair enough to remind them that a substantial reward had been offered for information, and that such an offer often tempted people to exaggerate or falsify evidence. He stressed that if there were any doubts in the jurors' minds, then the prisoners should be given the benefit of that doubt. Once again he questioned the admissibility of the evidence obtained by Jackson, saying that it was quite beyond the limits of duty of a constable to go into examinations and re-examinations of a remanded prisoner. He eventually ruled that Jackson's evidence was admissible, while cautioning him against obtaining a confession by such means in the future.

The judge pointed out that the statement obtained by Jackson could only affect James, since it was he who had confessed; it could not be considered as evidence against William. He also stated that he thought that it was improper for a gaoler to go from prisoner to prisoner to get evidence, so he had disallowed part of Dungey's testimony against James. Next the judge reiterated the evidence of Rouncevell and Mary Carveth for the benefit of the jury, stating that, if true, it made a strong case for suggesting that William could not have been seen in Bodmin at 4 p.m. on the afternoon of the murder.

Despite these wise words, the jury deliberated for only two minutes before finding both defendants guilty, and it was left to the judge to don his black cap and order that they each be hanged by the neck until dead. He urged the prisoners to prepare immediately to meet their God and to spend what little time remaining to them appeasing their offended Maker.

The Lightfoot brothers remained seemingly unconcerned at their fate. James asked to address the court in order explain how he had been drawn into the situation by his brother, whereas William was heard to ask for refreshments. Even after they had been taken to Bodmin Gaol, they still showed little concern for their situation and certainly no remorse, despite both having expressed regret for the murder in their earlier confessions to the magistrates. They acknowledged that the robbery of Mr Derry on the day before the murder of Mr Norway and the fact that the robbers had escaped detection had inspired them to commit a similar crime in order to obtain money. They also admitted to being heavy drinkers and to indulging in petty crime, with William putting his troubles down to 'bad company and keeping unholy the Lord's Day'. Meanwhile James confessed to having stolen the pistol from a Mrs Kendall of Mawgan, a statement that seemed at odds with the previous assertions of both brothers that they had never before committed highway robbery or robbed either a man or a house.

During their imprisonment in Bodmin, the brothers were in close contact with the prison chaplain to whom William promised a full confession. In the end none was forthcoming and William took the truth of Nevell Norway's murder with him to the grave. On the day before the brothers were hanged, the chaplain conducted a service in the prison chapel during which he asked the other prisoners to pray for their souls, pointing out that they could still enter heaven should they truly repent. Among the prisoners, only William and James showed no emotion at this service, although guards later heard William exhorting his brother from his cell to pray, and both men were observed kneeling in the early hours of the morning on which they were condemned to die.

The day of the execution saw Bodmin deluged by a constant stream of would-be spectators. Fearing a riot, authorities distributed notices entreating people to behave decently and maintain order. Meanwhile, the condemned men ate a hearty breakfast before leaving final messages for their wives and being led to the scaffold in chains. On their way to the gallows, they paused to shake hands with assembled dignitaries.

James was visibly afraid and trembling, but drew strength from his older brother who, as the rope was placed around his neck and the cap pulled over his eyes, again reminded James to pray. He then called for Parson Cole to come to his side, telling him 'I die happy' and asking to be remembered to his wife and family who, he hoped, he would meet again in heaven. Finally William beseeched his family to shun the paths of vice, not to break the Sabbath and to attend church regularly. When asked if he had anything to say, James too asked to be remembered to his wife and child and urged them to go to church.

These were the brothers' last words. The Lord's Prayer was recited and the chaplain made one last appeal to the Almighty to grant the sinners salvation. At this, the signal was given to the executioner to proceed. The bodies were displayed to the public for one hour before being cut down and buried without ceremony in the coal yard at the front of the prison.

It seems as though both men had seen highway robbery as an easy way of making money. After the attack on Mr Derry, they were, as William put it in his confession 'determined to enrich ourselves by similar means.' Whether they intended to go as far as actually killing someone is debatable. As William wrote, James visited his house on the day after the murder, saying; 'Dear me, Mr Norway's killed!' However, since they were known to the victim, it is probable that his death was the only way to ensure his silence.

Anecdotal evidence after the execution indicated that the brothers had already committed at least one other highway robbery. A labourer returning home from work was accosted by the brothers and relieved of his week's wages – the sum of 9s. The victim pleaded with his attackers not to take all of the money, as without it his wife and family would starve. Eventually the robbers agreed to give him back 2s, at which the labourer ran for home as fast as he possibly could. Soon he became aware that his attackers were following him. He quickly hid, hearing them pass by cursing and shouting, threatening to kill him if they could catch him. When the coast was clear, the labourer emerged from his hiding place and, on arriving home, was astonished to find that his attackers had mistakenly given him two sovereigns instead of 2s.

Perhaps the strangest aspect of the case is the uncannily accurate prediction of the murder by the victim's brother who, despite being thousands of miles away, 'saw' the whole scenario played out in a dream. The only difference between the content of the dream and what actually happened was the positioning of a house, which mysteriously moved from one side of the road to the other. It later emerged that since Edmund Norway's last visit to the scene, the layout of the road and been changed and the cottage he recalled so well *had* moved from the right to the left-hand side of the road.

Nevell Norway left behind a widow, Sarah, and six children unprovided for, but a subscription of £3,500 was made for their use, a noble testimony of the

The grave of Nevell Norway, the 'Merchant of Wadebridge', in Egloshayle churchyard near Wadebridge. (© Nicola Sly)

generous feeling of the public and the high estimation in which his amiable and spotless character was held. Sarah, who was also his first cousin, did not long survive her husband. Three years younger than him, she died at the age of thirty-six on 6 August 1840, the cause being recorded on her death certificate as 'hart [*sic*] disease'. Husband and wife are buried together in the churchyard at Egloshayle, about one mile from Wadebridge. Reflecting the esteem in which Norway was held in the area, the inscription on the headstone of their joint grave reads: 'Sacred to the memory of Nevell Norway, Merchant of Wadebridge, aged 39 years, murdered on 8 February 1840.'

The six children were all below the age of nine. The eldest, Arthur, was to become the grandfather of Nevil Shute Norway, who published several novels as Nevil Shute. In 1942 another novelist, John Rowland, published *The Death of Nevill* Norway,* a work of faction which Shute made an unsuccessful attempt to have suppressed on the grounds of privacy.

* In various contemporary accounts of the murder, the victim's forename is alternatively spelled Nevill.

7

'SEE WHAT A WRETCHED END I HAVE COME TO'

Camelford, 1844

Rough Tor, which lies on the fringes of Bodmin Moor, can be a bleak and desolate place, often shrouded in thick mists and low cloud. Dominated by Brown Willy, the highest natural peak in Cornwall, it is a wilderness broken only by granite outcrops, grazed by sheep and a few hardy moorland ponies. A shallow stream provides a source of drinking water for the animal inhabitants and close to this stream can be seen a sturdy granite monolith, marking the site of the tragic murder in 1844 of a young servant girl, Charlotte Dymond.

Charlotte was born in the nearby coastal village of Boscastle. Although her real parentage has never been reliably established, she was rumoured to be the illegitimate daughter of the village schoolmistress. If this was true, it had the potential to cause a scandal of epic proportions in such a small, close-knit village. The untimely birth of a daughter to a woman of such high social standing in the community would explain why young Charlotte, her very presence causing her mother untold embarrassment, was placed in service at the earliest possible age. Her first position was as a maid at Penhale Farm near Davidstow, owned by a 61-year-old widow, Phillippa Peter, who ran the holding with the assistance of her 38-year-old son, John. Here Charlotte met farm labourer, Matthew Weekes.

Six years older than Charlotte, Matthew could hardly be described as a good catch. By all accounts he was short, with a heavily pockmarked face caused by a childhood bout of smallpox, a pronounced limp and several missing teeth which gave him a permanent expression somewhere between a smirk and leer. He compensated for his appearance by dressing much more flamboyantly than would be expected of a farm labourer of the period, favouring velvet jackets and fancy waistcoats. His interest in clothes was one that he shared with Charlotte who, despite her lowly status, took great pride in her appearance, often adorning herself with scarves, beads and other trinkets. Although sometimes described as shy, Charlotte liked to make herself as attractive as possible to the opposite sex and was not averse to some gentle flirting on occasions.

Even if Matthew was not the most handsome man in the neighbourhood, he was steady and thrifty with his wages, and when Charlotte left to take up employment at another farm nearby, they began formally walking out together. Soon, to Matthew's delight, Charlotte returned to work at Penhale Farm where their relationship flourished – until an old workmate of Matthew's, Thomas Prout, arrived on the scene. Both men soon started arguing and Thomas threatened to steal Charlotte's affections. Harsh words were exchanged, and the situation worsened when Charlotte was given notice to quit by her employer. Matthew must have felt as though his world was falling apart.

In the event Charlotte did not leave her employment, mainly because she had nowhere else to go. Yet while still living under the same roof as Matthew, she was seen in animated conversation with his bitter rival. Earlier that morning, Matthew had been in high spirits, teasing Charlotte with a letter which he held just out of her reach. Now the sight of his beloved Charlotte together with Thomas sent him into a state of jealous agitation.

Shortly after talking with Prout, Charlotte dressed herself in her best clothes and left Penhale. It was late afternoon on Sunday 14 April 1844 when she tried to sneak away for a secret tryst. Challenged by her employer, Mrs Peter, who was determined to find out where she was going so late in the day, Charlotte managed to evade the question before leaving, closely followed by Matthew, also dressed in his Sunday best and carrying an umbrella to protect them both from the rain.

Matthew was expected to be back in good time to do the evening milking. However it was 9.30 p.m. when he returned to the farm alone. Asked where Charlotte was, he mumbled that he did not know and soon found himself facing a barrage of questions from Mrs Peter as to Charlotte's whereabouts. Mrs Peter stayed up waiting for Charlotte long after Weekes had retired for the night but, by milking time the following morning, she still had not returned.

According to Matthew, he had only walked with Charlotte for a little way before they parted company. Alone, he had walked to nearby Hallworthy, intending to visit the Westlake family, but on his arrival, everyone except Sally Westlake had been out. Over the next few days, under intense questioning, he first suggested that Charlotte might have run off with Thomas Prout. Finally he told 'the truth' – Charlotte had taken up another position working for Mrs Peter's niece in Blisland. The letter offering her the position was the very one that he had been teasing her with on the morning of her disappearance. Concerned, Mrs Peter pointed out that Blisland was a 10-mile walk across the moors and, having set out so late in the afternoon, Charlotte could not possibly have reached her intended destination by nightfall. At this, Matthew argued that Charlotte could have stayed overnight with a neighbour, Cain Speare, who lived at Brown Willy, before resuming her journey in the morning.

Over the next few days, Matthew was the subject of much speculation by local people who suggested that he might have harmed Charlotte to prevent his rival from having her. Gossip and rumour abounded in the small community, until Mrs Peter felt obliged to tackle him once more on the subject of Charlotte's mysterious disappearance. Once again he managed to evade her questions by retiring to his bed, ignoring her parting remark: 'Matthew, I am quite frightened. If you have hurted [sic] the girl, you ought to be hung in chains.' When a Mr Bethson asked

Matthew what he had done with the girl, the answer was, 'I don't know where she is gone, but if she is found murdered, they will take up her mother for it, for she said she would kill her if she came home again.' Though her mother's aversion to her daughter was well known, nobody thought for a moment that the former would be responsible for her murder.

A worried Mrs Peter waited until Matthew was out tending bullocks in the yard the following morning before asking her son John and another labourer, John Stevens, to check the facts as he had related them. Exactly one week after Charlotte had last been seen, the two men set off to Brown Willy and Blisland in pursuit of the truth. Seeing them leave, Matthew must have got wind of their errand. He went immediately to his bedroom and once again changed into his best clothes before leaving the farm, refusing to answer questions on where he was going, but promising to be back in time for supper that evening.

Meanwhile Mrs Peter's daughter, Mary Westlake, came to visit her mother and effectively broke Matthew's alibi. He had not visited the Westlake family as he had claimed. Now even more concerned for the safety of her maid, Mrs Peter and her daughter decided to search Matthew's belongings. To their horror, they found a handkerchief belonging to Charlotte in the pocket of the jacket he had worn on the day of her disappearance. They also found his heavily mud-stained trousers and a badly torn shirt that had been clumsily mended. A day or two earlier, Matthew had asked John Stevens, one of the other servants, for a needle and thread to sew a button to his shirt collar. John expressed surprise as the garment was a new one, but Matthew said it had been badly sewn. When Mrs Peter examined the shirt she found that it was not only new, but of good quality and particularly strong. She also found several spots of blood on the sleeve.

By nightfall, there was still no sign of Matthew. However John Peter and John Stevens returned with distressing news; there had been no offer of a job and Charlotte had not stayed at either Blisland or Brown Willy. Not until the following Tuesday morning, nine days after Charlotte had vanished, was a search party organised. Acting on information from two local farmers, both of whom claimed to have seen a young woman accompanied by a man with a distinctive limping gait, they concentrated their search on the fringes of the moor where, almost miraculously considering the length of time that had passed, they identified a woman's footprints in the damp ground. Opposite were a man's footprints, close enough to suggest there might have been a struggle.

These prints led searchers to a marshy area near Rough Tor Ford, where Charlotte's body was soon discovered lying partially submerged in the stream, her throat slashed from ear to ear. Surrounded by pools of diluted blood, Charlotte lay with one arm stretched above her shoulder, the other by her side. One knee was bent upwards, part of her bodice had been torn away and her dress was raised above her knees with one of her stockings pulled halfway down her leg. Her treasured coral beads were scattered around her head.

A surgeon, Mr Good, was summoned to examine the body, which he loaded onto a cart, returning it to Penhale Farm where it was placed in an outbuilding. After a more detailed examination of Charlotte's body, the surgeon concluded that she had died as the result of the horrific wound on her neck which, he surmised, had been caused by a rather blunt knife or similar cutting instrument.

Rough Tor on the edge of Bodmin Moor, where Charlotte Dymond was killed in April 1844. (© Nicola Sly)

The stream on Rough Tor where Charlotte was killed. (© Nicola Sly)

He could not rule out the possibility that the wound had been self-inflicted, but felt it unlikely and he further stated that Charlotte was not pregnant, nor could he find any evidence of sexual assault.

Back on the moors, searchers were still combing the area for any trace of Charlotte's missing clothing. Her shawl, scarf, bonnet, shoes and the pattens that she had worn over her shoes to protect them from the mud were eventually found covered by moss, hidden in a bloodstained pit, almost half a mile from where her body was found. Her gloves and black silk handbag were still missing.

Several miles away, the prime suspect Matthew Weekes was visiting old friends at Coad's Green. His friends found him pensive, preoccupied and uncharacteristically reticent when it came to answering questions about his beloved Charlotte. When the young daughter of the house proudly boasted about owning a handbag, Matthew briefly produced a lace-trimmed black bag from his own pocket to show her.

Local police were already on Matthew's trail. Aware that he had relatives in Plymouth, Constable John Bennett hastened to the city and, quite by chance, bumped into Matthew on Plymouth Hoe, accompanied by his sister and her husband. He was immediately taken to Hallworthy Inn, Davidstow, where a search of his person located the missing gloves concealed in his jacket pockets. On this discovery he was charged with Charlotte's murder and summoned to appear before 'King John', the magistrate John King Lethbridge. He was then escorted in a cart to Camelford, then a gig to Bodmin, where he was committed to gaol to await his trial.

Numerous witnesses now came forward to testify that they had seen the couple on the moor that fateful Sunday afternoon. Although their accounts did not conclusively prove that the sightings had been of Matthew and Charlotte, the circumstantial evidence against Weekes was persuasive. Besides, he had effectively been condemned by gossip and innuendo, even before Charlotte's terrible fate was known.

Matthew was not allowed to give his own version of events in court, but maintained his composure in the face of a guilty verdict from the foreman of the jury. Only when the judge pronounced the death sentence did he react at all, slumping backwards in a faint, before being carried unconscious from the courtroom by two guards.

While awaiting his execution, Matthew seemed ashamed at having brought such disgrace to his family. In contrition he allegedly made a full confession, stating that he and Charlotte had initially walked together making idle conversation. Then he had jealously accused his girlfriend of behaving disgracefully with another man and, to his horror, the woman he loved so much had turned her back on him, retorting that she would do as she pleased and had nothing more to say on the subject. At this he had seen red, pulling out his pocketknife and lunging at her. Even then, he maintained that he had come to his senses and put the knife away without harming her and that it was only when she repeated her remarks that he lashed out again, this time with fatal consequences. Panic-stricken by the sight of Charlotte's body toppling to the ground, blood gushing from her neck, he had quickly hidden her clothes and fled, discarding the bloodstained knife as he ran.

Charlotte Dymond's grave, St David's Church, Davidstow. (© Nicola Sly)

A memorial to Charlotte Dymond, erected on Rough Tor near the scene of her murder. (© Nicola Sly)

In Bodmin Gaol, the illiterate Matthew dictated two letters which he signed with his cross. In one, he asked his family to distribute his few personal belongings and urged his brothers to adopt a more Christian way of life. He addressed the second letter to his former employer, Mrs Peter, forgiving her for standing as a witness against him and thanking her for her kindness to him. He also thanked the judge and jury for giving him his just desserts and the chaplain for his endeavours to save his soul. And, in both letters, he made an impassioned plea to other young men and women not to place too much trust in the opposite sex, saying; 'See what a wretched end I have come to by loving too much'.

Weekes was executed at Bodmin Gaol before a crowd of almost 20,000 spectators on 12 August 1844. His body was suspended by the neck for the customary one hour and one minute, before being cut down and buried without ceremony in an unmarked grave in the prison grounds. Yet he was immortalised, forever tied to his true love by the wording inscribed on the granite monument, erected by public contribution, that still marks the site of her tragic demise:

This monument was erected by public subscription in memory of Charlotte Dymond who was murdered here by Matthew Weekes on Sunday April 14 1844

The two lovers are also commemorated in a poem, *The Ballad of Charlotte Dymond* by Charles Causley.

8

'HOLD YOUR NOISE, OR I WILL GIVE YOU A SLAP'

Launceston, 1878

Selina Wadge had two young sons, Johnny aged five and Harry aged two, both born out of wedlock. Harry was partly crippled and had great difficulty in standing or walking very far. Selina's future prospects did not look very bright, until she met a young bachelor, James Westwood, who had spent fifteen years in the army and was now a labourer. They fell in love and became engaged, but she told others that he had agreed to marry her only on condition that she 'get rid' of the younger boy. When the time came, he would firmly deny having said any such thing.

Selina had been an inmate of the Union Workhouse at Launceston for about a year when she left on 8 July 1878 to go and live with her father at Trebant, about seven miles away. On the morning of Friday 21 July, she and the children were seen riding into Launceston in a farmer's wagon, where they were left in the town. Not long afterwards she was noticed walking towards a field about one and a half miles away from the town centre. By midday she was back in the town, but now she only had the elder boy with her.

When she returned to the workhouse her widowed sister Mary Ann Boundry came to call and asked what had happened to the younger boy. 'Harry was dead and buried,' she said, 'he died of an abscess and the throat complaint.' She had a doctor to come and call on him, she added, and they got a coffin for him; she and the doctor buried the boy between them, by the church door at Altarnun.

'He's in a pit, mother,' the other boy piped up.

'Hold your noise, or I will give you a slap,' she retorted.

That night she slept at a lodging house in Launceston where the landlady, Harriet Parker, asked after her baby. Selina replied that he had died of a throat complaint at her mother's house, but she had been prepared for it, as the doctor had warned her that he was so ill that she should not hold out any hope for his recovery.

On Saturday 22 July she went back to the workhouse. As she and her boys had been well known in the area, people were beginning to become suspicious. Next day, when questioned by the matron and others as to what had happened to the younger child, she changed her story again. She told them that Mr Westwood had taken him from her and thrown him down a well. He had threatened to do the same with the elder boy, but she had run away from him in time. They were not convinced, and she subsequently broke down, confessing that she had put him in the well. Nobody else apart from the elder boy was with her at the time, she admitted, and he cried bitterly when he saw what she had done.

On behalf of the police, Superintendent Sheraton went to check the well that afternoon and found the child's body. George Wilson, a surgeon from Launceston, confirmed that death had been caused by suffocation, and that the appearance of the body suggested that he had drowned. There was no sign of any abscess or throat disease.

Selina Wadge was tried at Bodmin Assizes on 27 July, with Mr Clark and Mr Templar prosecuting, and Mr Massey for the defence.

Several witnesses were called by the prosecution. One of the first was William Holman, a farmer from Altarnun, who said he drove the prisoner and her children to Launceston. She had told him she was going to visit Mr Westwood, who was coming from Stratton to meet her. As they passed the well at Mowhay Park, she said, 'I see the well is railed off now.' The fact that she had drawn attention to this point would later prove crucial. He dropped them off at the entrance to the town, about a mile beyond the well.

A little later Richard Langman, a wagoner, noticed Selina and the boys near the field with the well. Emmanuel Chudleigh, who farmed this field, told the court that the well was covered with boards and railed off. That same Friday he noticed that the boards had been moved and not put back properly as he had done on the previous night, but a cursory examination of the well itself revealed nothing more than a little froth on the water, so he had no reason to suspect anything.

The next three witnesses were from the Launceston workhouse. Jane Pethick, a schoolmistress, said that she had seen the prisoner in the house, and the latter had told her that she had just lost her little boy to throat disease. When Louisa Downing, the matron, questioned her further, she broke down and confessed what she had done; 'I did it, but he put me up to it.' When asked who 'he' was, she mentioned a name – presumably Westwood – which Mrs Downing did not remember. She admitted to having put Harry in the water; 'there was no one with me at the time but little Johnny and he began to cry.' Mary Pooley, another of the matrons, said that little Johnny had made a statement to her. 'Mother put Harry in a pit; there was no one there and Harry cried.'

Police Sergeant Barrett had interviewed the prisoner at the workhouse. She told him that she met a man and took him towards Tresmarrow Road. At the time she had both children with her. The man picked up the smaller boy, ran into a field with him, then came out and said he had thrown him in a pit where there were some railings and drowned him. This same man said he would drown her and the elder boy, whereupon she took to her heels and ran away, taking the boy with her. This man was Westwood.

Next in the witness box was Harriet Parker, at whose lodgings the prisoner had stayed on the night of 21 July. She was followed by Sergeant Roseveare, who produced the clothes the dead child was wearing when found. His colleague Superintendent Sheraton described finding the body in the well.

Evidence was clearly mounting against Selina Wadge, even before James Westwood got up to address the court. He said that he first met her on 15 December 1877, again on 26 March 1878, and then not again until about a month previously, on 29 June. He had been working in the parish of Morwenstow during the week ending 22 June. Being engaged to her, he was well aware that she had two illegitimate children, but he did not object to them in the least. He had always been fond of them and often spoken to them in a kind and affectionate manner. Not once did he suggest that they would be 'encumbrances' to them as husband and wife, and there was nothing to suggest that he would not have been a good stepfather. On 22 June he had meant to wait for Selina at the turnpike gate on Bodmin Road near Launceston, but work commitments prevented him from keeping the appointment.

Was James Westwood the guilty party, and was he using Selina Wadge as a catspaw, or was she playing a clever game, posing as a poor mother at the mercy of a wicked fiancé? One of them was lying, and if it was Selina then she was doing her best to blacken James' good name. Constable Armstrong told the court that while she was in custody, Selina had told him she was going away with Westwood, 'and he was going to marry me if I could get rid of one of the children.' After a pause, she added, 'I tried to get in after it; I tried with a kibble (a large iron bucket used by Cornish miners). Oh! My poor mother, it will break her heart.' This concluded the case for the prosecution.

There were no witnesses for the defence, but Mr Massey argued persuasively on his client's behalf. He said that the prosecution believed the prisoner had planned the murder; she had arranged to ride to the spot she had chosen with both her children, one of whom was said to be a sprightly, intelligent child, very forward for his age; and that when they passed the field in which the well stood and in which she had decided to throw the child, she called the wagon driver's attention to the fact that railings had been placed around it. She could perfectly well have left the elder boy in Launceston or at home, instead of taking him with her to be a witness to the deed; she could have said that the younger boy had tumbled into the well, and there would have been nobody in a position to contradict her. In the light of all these events, it was highly improbable that the prisoner would have carried out such a barbarous and unnatural murder. Mr Westwood had told the court how fond he was of children, and that he never objected to them. Did anyone believe that he would have carried out the murder himself?

The prisoner, he went on, had lied 'in a moment of great excitement', but that in itself could not be taken as evidence of guilt. Many an innocent person might be hanged if the telling of a lie was taken as conclusive evidence against them. Moreover, witnesses for the prosecution had proved that the prisoner had always been a kind and affectionate mother to both children, particularly to the deceased, in view of his physical infirmity.

In summing up, Mr Justice Denman complimented Mr Massey on his defence, while remarking that he must take exception to a request made to the jury that 'if they had any doubt about the case they should give to the prisoner the benefit of it'. That, the judge said, was an expression frequently employed by counsel in defending prisoners; but in his view it was 'a fallacious and artful one, and intended to deceive juries'. The jury had no right to grant any benefit or boon to any one, but only to be just and do their duty. He then pointed out that even if Westwood had instigated the prisoner to commit the act, of which there was no evidence whatsoever, she would be just as guilty of murder. If the jury believed the prisoner's story to the extent that Westwood initiated it; that still made it an admission of murder on her part. He also referred to some letters written by Westwood to the prisoner which completely contradicted the charges made by her against him.

There was still some doubt, the judge added, as to whether Westwood had anything to do with the murder. If the prisoner had told the story falsely, it was not only a terrible case of 'foul murder', but also a wicked and serious charge for her to bring against him. If the jury thought it was proved that she was guilty of murder, he would not insult them by supposing that by any cowardice, weakness or folly, or false sentiment they would abstain from returning the verdict which the law required them to return. Should there be any reasonable doubt, it would be their duty to acquit the prisoner.

Throughout the proceedings Selina Wadge had seemed perfectly unmoved. The jury were out for just over half an hour and found her guilty, but recommended her to mercy on the grounds that the murder had not been premeditated, and because of the prisoner's previous love for her children. If it had not been premeditated, one would think that manslaughter might have been a rather more suitable verdict; but perhaps Selina Wadge's rather despicable attempt to evade responsibility by blaming James Westwood counted too heavily against her.

Mr Justice Denman sentenced her to death, adding that a recommendation to mercy would be forwarded to the proper quarter. Nevertheless she would do well not to hold out any great hope, but instead to prepare herself for death. She wept bitterly as she was assisted out of the dock, but while awaiting the sentence to be carried out she confessed to the murder and 'admitted the justice of her sentence'.

On 15 August Selina Wadge, aged twenty-eight, was executed by William Marwood at Bodmin Gaol. This time the people of Cornwall were deprived of what had been their customary entertainment, if it could be termed as such. It was the first death sentence to be carried out in the county for sixteen years, and according to *The Times*, 'this being consequently the first since the abolition of public executions, there was a great deal of curiosity as to the proceedings; but the curious were disappointed, for the execution was conducted with the strictest privacy, even the representatives of the Press being denied admission.'

9

'IT IS WELL TAKEN CARE OF'

Lanlivery, 1882

Four years after Selina Wadge had paid the ultimate penalty for killing an apparently unwanted infant, a reluctant father was convicted of a similar offence.

William Meager Bartlett was a foreman at the Calcarrow granite works near St Blazey. A married man with seven children, he was aged forty-five when he became a father for the eighth time in the late summer of 1881. However, he could not resist a fling with the nurse who attended Mrs Bartlett during her last pregnancy. The nurse, a widow, Elizabeth Anne Wherry, subsequently discovered she was carrying his child. By the spring of 1882 she and the father-to-be could no longer conceal the fact. Neither of them wanted Mrs Bartlett to know.

In April 1882 she went to Newquay 'to avoid exposure' and on 4 June she gave birth to a daughter, whom she named Emma Owen. The baby was put out to another nurse, Mrs Knight, who lived in the house next door to where Mrs Wherry had had her confinement in Newquay. Before Mrs Wherry had left, Bartlett had given her some envelopes so she could write to him with regard to the matter of bringing the child back afterwards but keeping her away from the public gaze. The envelopes did not contain his full name, just 'William Meager, care of Thomas Philp, Packhorse Hill, St Blazey'.

On 22 June the baby was taken by Ellen Knight, with a feeding bottle, a bundle of clothes and an inventory of the same made by Mrs Wherry, to Par station. This had been done at Mrs Wherry's request, as a result of orders from Bartlett. Calling himself Mr Meager, he met Mrs Knight at Par at about 1 p.m. that day. They walked a short distance from the station, and met William Philp and his wife Annie, to whom the child was given, Bartlett saying that Mrs Philp was the nurse. Some conversation took place concerning the feeding of the baby, and then Mrs Knight left the baby, the clothes and bottle with the Philps.

A few days before this happened, Bartlett had seen William Philp, a workman in the toolhouse at the quarry, and told him he had received a letter from an old friend of his about an illegitimate child. He had therefore arranged to take the child and have it nursed, and he needed Philp and his wife to be near Par station on 22 June to take the child home and look after it for a few hours, then meet him again with it at 3 p.m. at Old Drum Hill, near Bartlett's office. By then he would have a trap and horse ready to take it to a place 10 miles away, where it was to be nursed.

Philp agreed to this, and in letters written by Bartlett to Mrs Wherry, it was shown that he had pretended to her that a Mrs Philp had agreed to take the baby and nurse it for 2s 6d per week. The Philps returned soon after 3 p.m., when Bartlett met them and said that the people had been waiting some time. He took the bundle of clothes and went with it to his office, some sixty yards away. On returning he gave Philp a bottle of stout and his wife an envelope containing 5s for helping, and then took the baby with its feeding bottle.

It was the last time anybody else saw the baby alive. Mrs Wherry left Newquay on 29 June, and met Bartlett a few days afterwards. When she asked him where the child was he said, 'You don't know,' assuring her that 'It is well taken care of.'

On 3 July Joseph Rundle, an employee at the granite works, saw Bartlett being dragged out of a large pool near the quarry by several people; he had evidently been on the point of drowning. At first they thought he was rinsing out some equipment, had lost his balance and fallen in. However the water was only about 4ft deep at most, and for some distance from the bank it gradually sloped down, so had he fallen in he would have had no difficulty in getting himself out. But when his helpers rescued him he was looking shattered, and repeatedly asked to be left alone, saying, 'Let me die'. His falling in was clearly no accident.

Why, people and police began to wonder, should William Bartlett want to kill himself? Could there be any connection between this and the rumours that a baby had been born in the area, or at least born to somebody in the area, but had since disappeared?

Two days later Philp told Bartlett that people were starting to gossip, and he wanted to know where the child was. Bartlett replied that he would not tell. When Philp pressed him, Bartlett snapped that it was no business of his and that he would not be mixed up in the matter, as he (Bartlett) had not said which Philp it was who had the child, there being another family of the same name in the town. When the police started questioning Bartlett, he was a little less evasive. 'I promised not to tell anything about it and I never shall; I gave a party a lump sum to take the child away, and it is well cared for. I have sent it to London.'

Another policeman, Inspector Richard Nicholls, asked Bartlett what had happened to the child. 'Oh, it's at the house of Mr Philp.' 'That's all right,' answered Nicholls. 'Yes, that's all right,' Bartlett added, 'but don't go and say anything about it, because it will cause surprise among the neighbours.' Yet Nicholls had his doubts, and he advised his colleagues that it would probably be necessary to search the area before long.

In the course of their enquiries, on 7 July the police visited Bartlett's office at the granite works, where they found a bundle of clothes, and all the garments were identified by Mrs Wherry and Mrs Knight as those sent with the baby from Newquay. If the child had been sent to London, as he had maintained, it was reasonable to suppose that the clothes would have gone there too. After asking questions among the other staff, the police learnt that up to 22 June there used to be two small boxes similar to the one found, in the prisoner's office, but now there was only one.

Next morning PC Yeo volunteered to go and look down a disused mine shaft at Colkerrow, overgrown with brambles and general undergrowth, near the quarry tramway, and about forty yards from the office. Despite the risks inherent from foul air and gas, he was convinced he would find something as he searched below with a small light. After going some way down he found the mark of a man's knee or boot part of the way down the shaft, followed by a large heap of stones in one of the levels, and began to move them. They revealed a box lying on some straw. It had been nailed down, and as he opened it he found the dead and very decomposed body of a baby girl. The corpse was dressed exactly like Mrs Wherry's baby had been clothed on the day it left Newquay, and had dark hair.

Bartlett was arrested, and kept his silence. On 9 July a post-mortem on the body of Emma Owen Wherry was carried out by the surgeon Thomas Tuckey, who decided that she must have been dead for several days as the body was in an advanced state of decomposition. A piece of string and a woman's corset lace were found tied tightly round the child's neck. In his opinion, these must have been put on when the child was alive, and the cause of death was strangulation. That same day a baby's feeding bottle, about half full of milk, was found hidden in a hole on a rocky ledge behind Bartlett's office.

After being held in custody for nearly three weeks, Bartlett appeared at Bodmin Assizes on 29 July before Lord Justice Lindley. Still looking far from well, he pleaded 'Not Guilty' in what a local reporter called 'a feeble voice'. Mr W. Molesworth St Aubyn and Mr J. Fortescue appeared for the prosecution, with Mr Collins and Mr Austin for the defence.

Mr St Aubyn read several extracts from letters sent by Bartlett to Mrs Wherry, revealing his intentions regarding moving the child away from Newquay. In one of the letters he said he had spoken to a party about meeting the midday train at Par, that he had arranged that after the child had been 'turned over' the woman who took it 'should go her way, and the one who brought it he would accompany back to the station', and that the parties he had spoken to had no idea whose child it was. They imagined that he was making the arrangements on behalf of somebody else.

Another letter was more specific. In it Bartlett wrote, 'I hope we will pull through all right. Philp's wife is going to take it, as she lost one about three months ago.' Later he had added, 'I hope on Tuesday to be able to send you a very favourable account of our arrangement. I know they have not the slightest idea where the child will come from.'

When cross-examined, Elizabeth Wherry confirmed that the clothes the baby had on when found in the box were the same as those in which she had been dressed the last time she saw her, and Ellen Knight testified to having attended Mrs Wherry in her confinement. She also recognised the clothes produced as those which had been sent with the child. William Philp gave evidence regarding his meeting Bartlett at Par station to take the child for a short time before someone else arrived to collect it, and his wife Annie confirmed the statement. Joseph Rundle spoke of seeing the prisoner after he had been rescued from the pool, telling his rescuers to leave him alone and let him die, and Inspector Nicholls gave evidence as to finding the bundle of clothes. Thomas Tuckey revealed the results of the post-mortem, saying that the child had been dead for several days.

He did not think decomposition was the cause of the appearance of the lungs and the heart, as the lungs might have been congested by other causes besides strangulation. When asked by Mr Collins if the strings had been tied very tightly, he said that the staylace was very tight, but the piece of twine appeared to have been put on afterwards.

The counsel for the prosecution and the defence both summed up in some detail. Mr Collins concluded by drawing the jury's attention to the fact that until the charge had been brought against him the prisoner 'had been a man of irreproachable character', and he proposed to call witnesses to testify to this. The Revd H. Taylor, vicar of Lostwithiel and former curate-in-charge at Lanlivery, a county magistrate and a local Methodist preacher, all appeared in the witness box to say they had known Bartlett for some time and believed him of good character.

The jury retired to consider their verdict at 3 p.m., and were recalled by the judge some four and a half hours later. The foreman said they were 'eleven agreed', but one juryman was not satisfied as to the identity of the body. As this was, in the judge's words, 'practically the whole question', the jury were asked to consider the matter again. A few minutes later the foreman told him that 'we are not likely to agree from what I can see of this juryman'.

'I cannot do more,' replied the judge, his patience running a little thin. 'I take it for granted no juryman came into the box determined not to agree. That would be too bad. I must ask you to retire.' Further conversation ensued, then the foreman repeated that there was no chance of their agreeing. The judge ordered them to retire again, and recalled them at 10 p.m. When told yet again that there was no chance of the jury agreeing, the judge admitted that he would 'only be performing an act of undue harshness' if he was to detain them any longer. Much as he regretted the result, he would have to discharge them. The prisoner would have to be tried again, either on Monday 31 July or at the next assizes.

On consulting the counsel for the prosecution and for the defence, Mr Collins said that in the interest of the prisoner he felt he ought not to ask for a new trial on Monday, and requested an adjournment. It was arranged that the prisoner would have to be remanded in custody until October, when the case could be heard at Exeter.

Bartlett duly faced a second court before Lord Justice Bowen on 27 October. Again, Mr Molesworth St Aubyn and Mr Fortescue were the prosecutors, and the Hon. Bernard Coleridge defended the prisoner at the request of the judge.

Once again Elizabeth Wherry and William Philp were called on as witnesses for the prosecution, as were several policemen, including Inspector Nicholls, Sergeant John Thomas, PCs Yeo and Kendall, and Superintendent Jago. After hearing the same evidence as produced in court at Bodmin almost three months earlier, Mr Coleridge pointed out that no concealment had been attempted, but every arrangement had been made that the child should be cared for. It was to be taken away, not to a sudden death, but to the charge of those who would care for it. The prisoner knew the police had got the bundle, and were searching for the child, yet he had made no effort to escape. Having asked the jury what evidence there was to connect the prisoner with the murder, Mr Coleridge suggested that the body found was not necessarily that of Mrs Wherry's child. It could, he said, have been abandoned by any woman in the neighbourhood wanting to get rid of an unwanted child. If it had been strangled partly by a woman's corset lace, a woman was more likely to be responsible; surely a man would not have such an object at his disposal? (Bartlett was a married man, which rather disposed of that argument.)

The major thrust of his defence, however, was the lack of new evidence, coupled with the fact that Bartlett had not been convicted at Bodmin. 'Was there anything now brought forward different from what had been brought forward before?' asked Coleridge. 'Was the jury that day (of the previous trial) more obstinate, foolish, wilful or criminal, and so stepped in to take up the trial for the prisoner's life?' If the last jury was not satisfied, why should the present jury think otherwise?

The court adjourned for thirty minutes, and returned with a verdict of Guilty. In summing up, the judge remarked that the previous jury's inability to agree did not amount to an acquittal, especially as only one man had stood in the way of a unanimous verdict. Above all, it was in the prisoner's power to produce the infant if still alive. Thanking the jurors, he concluded, 'I do not see how honest men, in the discharge of their duty as jurymen, could come to any other verdict.'

As the death sentence was pronounced, Bartlett was helped from the dock. He went to the gallows at Bodmin on 13 November, where he was hanged by William Marwood.

10

'I WILL SOON SETTLE THE LOT OF YOU'

Penzance, 1886

One summer day in 1886 the people of Penzance were shocked by an apparently inexplicable burst of violence on the part of one man which left four people dead.

James Hawke, George Gerrard and his wife Elizabeth, and Charles Uren and his wife Mary had been friends for some time. On the morning of 28 July 1886, James Hawke was at the Navy Inn, Penzance, where he had two glasses of beer. Thomas Blewett, the landlord, had a friend from London with him and they were planning to go out in a boat together. Blewett invited Hawke to join them, and all three went for a short cruise about an hour later. Hawke seemed perfectly normal at the time, and he steered the boat part of the way out of the harbour for them.

Early in the afternoon he went to the Urens' house in Marine Terrace. George Gerrard, a watch and instrument repairer who kept a shop in Daniel Place, had called round as Uren had a clock and an accordion which needed repair. His wife was passing, and a friend told her he was there, so she called in to see him. Hawke still seemed in a normal temper, and sat down in a chair to chat happily to them for about five minutes. Nobody thought for a moment that he was drunk. However, he got up and left for a while, and when he returned he was clearly in a bad mood. On coming back into the house, he said, 'If you do not clear out from here I will soon settle the lot of you,' and went upstairs.

Feeling uneasy, George Gerrard asked Elizabeth to leave as he thought Hawke was up to no good. While in the yard he heard two shots, and begged her to come away at once. Instead, she went back to the door and Hawke confronted her. 'I have said nothing to you,' she told him. This, everyone thought, referred to a previous conversation which Hawke must have found disagreeable for some reason. Without replying, he produced a revolver and shot her twice, killing her instantly. Sensing that he would be in danger if he was in the wrong place at the wrong time, George had made himself scarce.

The Urens' next-door neighbour, Rebecca Roberts, had known Hawke for over twenty years. She normally saw him two or three times a day, and regarded him as a friend. At about 1.45 p.m. she was at the back of her house when she heard something which sounded to her like boys in the lane letting off crackers. She went to her window and saw a woman lying in the yard. She went to the door,

The Promenade, Penzance.

saw Hawke in the doorway and asked him what he had done. At first he did not reply and she was about to shut her door when he called her, and took a purse from his trousers and a watch from his waistcoat pocket which he put in her hands. 'Give them to Clara,' he told her. Clara was the daughter of Charles Uren by his first wife. He then shook hands with Mrs Roberts, and said goodbye to her 'as coolly as if he had been going on a journey'. He then raised the pistol to his head, fired and fell dead.

The medical evidence showed that Mr Uren and Mrs Gerrard had been killed with two bullets, and Mrs Uren one. Richard Nicholas, Superintendent of the Penzance Borough Police, said that when he took charge of the revolver, five barrels had been reloaded.

John Rescorla, the borough coroner, held an inquest at Penzance Guildhall on the next morning. The first witness to be called was Thomas Blewett, who confirmed the details of Hawke's appearance at the Navy Inn and the boat trip afterwards. Hawke, he confirmed, had been in a good mood – ''e appeared just the same as usual' – and did not appear to have a weapon with him.

John Searle, a waterman at Marine Place, said he saw the three go out in the boat, and noticed nothing peculiar about Hawke. At about 1.30 p.m. he saw Hawke in conversation with Thomas Daniell, wheelwright, and others, in front of Daniell's premises in Queen Street. Hawke left after a while and went to chat to some people near the Marine Retreat for a few minutes, before going to the Urens' house. Soon after that he heard another shot. He ran in the direction from whence they came, and when he came to Marine Place he saw Mrs Gerrard lying in the yard, apparently dead. Hawke was standing in the door. 'Who has committed this crime?' Searle asked. Hawke did not reply, but took the items from his pockets to give to Mrs Roberts, said goodbye to her, put the pistol to his head, fired, and fell down. Searle took the pistol from him and handed it to PC Cliff who was there.

Mrs Roberts gave her version of events, adding that after Hawke said goodbye to her she went back to her house, shut the door, 'and saw nothing more'. 'Did you not think it was a strange circumstance?' the coroner asked. 'Yes, I did.'

'And yet you coolly went away and shut your door?'

'I went away because someone said he had shot the woman, and I was afraid.'

George Gerrard was next. He confirmed that he and his wife were on excellent terms with Hawke, that he had been to the Urens' house about a dozen times, and that when Hawke came into the house at first he 'appeared quite cool and agreeable in his manner'. Only after he went out and came back did he behave as if he was 'in a passion'. He had warned his wife that Hawke was 'up to some roguery, let us clear out.' 'You mean by "roguery" violence?' asked the Coroner. 'Yes.'

Another man, Mr Wermot, a diver, had been passing when the shots were fired. He rushed at Hawke in order to try and restrain him from any further mischief, a rather foolhardy move, but was too late to stop him from killing himself with one more shot.

Richard Nicholas, Superintendent of the Penzance Borough Police, reported that he had been called to the Urens' house, and saw Mrs Gerrard lying on her right side in the yard apparently dead, blood oozing through her dress at the back. Going towards the front door of the house he saw Hawke lying on his back, bleeding from a wound on the right side of his head. In the kitchen he found the body of Charles Uren, and with her head on the back door step that of his wife.

In conclusion, the Coroner said that all the evidence showed great deliberation on Hawke's part, and that he had killed three people in cold blood before putting the weapon to his own head. He could not offer any reasons for Hawke's motives in doing so. The jury returned a verdict of wilful murder with respect to Charles and Mary Uren and Elizabeth Gerrard, and of *felo de se* or suicide against Hawke with respect to himself. What had suddenly turned an apparently normal, sober man whom so many people had known as a friend for so long into a multiple killer would never be known.

11

MURDER IN FALMOUTH HARBOUR

Falmouth, 1886, 1887 & 1901

Within the space of fifteen years, three murders took place at sea not far from Falmouth. All had various factors in common, though in each case the outcome was to be different.

The first took place aboard the Nova Scotian barque *Nicosia*, which sailed into Falmouth docks on Friday 31 January 1886, under the command of Captain McDonald. On board, restrained in heavy chains, was Mexican seaman Antonio Sach, who it was alleged had stabbed the ship's second mate, Harry Wilson, causing his death. As soon as the ship docked, the harbour police were informed of the incident. After obtaining a warrant for Sach's arrest, they boarded the vessel and removed the Mexican to the town lock-up. He appeared before magistrates in Falmouth on the following Monday, charged with the wilful murder of Wilson.

According to the evidence produced in court, Sach had served aboard *Nicosia* for about a year and was generally thought of as a well-behaved and conscientious seaman. At about 4 a.m. on the morning of the murder Wilson, a native of Liverpool who was married with children, had given Sach an order to reduce the ship's sail. An argument had ensued between the two men and, in a moment of passion, Sach had unsheathed his knife and plunged it several times into Wilson's chest, in the area of his left breast.

Mortally wounded, Wilson managed to run towards the captain's cabin, shouting, 'The wretch has put a knife in me!' before collapsing dead onto the deck. Captain McDonald immediately disarmed Sach, who was still clutching the bloody knife. When asked if he had done it, Sach replied in the affirmative, adding that now the deceased would never strike another man.

Sach was committed for trial at Exeter Assizes, where his case opened before Mr Justice Day on 19 May 1886. Having heard all the evidence, Day took the unusual step of instructing the jury to return a verdict of manslaughter rather than murder, since he felt that the attack on Wilson had been committed in self-defence. Describing Wilson as 'a brutal man and a disgrace to the flag under which he sailed', Day reasoned that, while Sach's use of a knife could not be justified, there were extenuating circumstances, namely the prolonged bullying and violence, which he had suffered at the hands of the second mate. Accordingly,

Shipping in Falmouth Harbour.

the jury returned a verdict of manslaughter and Mr Justice Day passed a sentence of twelve months' imprisonment.

The following year, the 386-ton brig *Sant Antonio* docked in Falmouth harbour at about 9 a.m. on the morning of Friday 19 August 1887, carrying a cargo of linseed. Throughout her voyage from Rosario, Italy, a niggling quarrel had simmered between two of her crew members, chief mate Enrico Ciampa and cook Francesco Poggi.

After the boat had dropped anchor, the prolonged bad feeling between the two men boiled over and they began fighting, initially with bare fists, but it soon became more serious than that. At around midday Poggi pulled out a sheath knife, slashing into the jugular vein on the left-hand side of Ciampa's neck, and also cutting the left side of the chief mate's face.

The wound bled profusely. Ciampa was given immediate first aid by his shipmates and word was sent to the Italian consul Mr Fox, who immediately arranged for doctors to attend to the stricken seaman. Doctors Harris and Owen from Falmouth, accompanied by PC Sanders, boarded the ship at about 12.45 p.m. They went below decks to attend the victim, finding him 'all of a heap' at the foot of the companion ladder, but they were too late – Ciampa had bled to death.

Poggi had been restrained by the ship's crew members and was roped to a belaying pin on the port side of the main deck. He was promptly arrested by Constable Sanders and charged with Ciampa's murder. After spending the night securely detained in Falmouth's town lock-up, Poggi appeared before magistrates on the following morning, a Saturday. Claiming that he had acted in self-defence, Poggi demanded the services of an interpreter from Italy, promising that, when brought before a proper tribunal, he would reveal exactly what had happened and how Ciampa had ended up dead. The case was adjourned until Thursday 25 August.

Before re-opening the hearing, Poggi was examined by Dr Harris and Dr Moore on behalf of the Treasury. Following this examination, which was conducted in the presence of a Treasury solicitor, they pronounced Poggi insane. It was arranged that he should be transported to what was then known as Broadmoor Criminal Lunatic Asylum in Berkshire until arrangements could be made to hand him over to the Italian Government. Five of the crew of the *Sant Antonio* who had been detained in Falmouth as potential witnesses were allowed to leave, travelling to Hull in order to rejoin the ship.

In due course Mr Lewis from the Treasury travelled to Falmouth, bringing with him the necessary forms for committing the prisoner to an asylum under warrant of the Home Secretary. The solicitor for the Treasury, Mr Fox, notified magistrates that the forms had been received and the town Mayor, Mr Carter, magistrate Mr Solomon, Dr Harris and Dr Moore went to the lock-up where Poggi was still under detention and examined him. Having satisfied themselves that he was indeed insane, a certificate was signed in accordance with the Criminal Lunatic Act of 1884. The certificate was despatched to the Home Office, requesting that a warrant should be sent as soon as possible.

Pending the arrival of the warrant, Poggi was again formally remanded and the case against him adjourned.

The third murder involved the Liverpool-based ship *Lorton*, which set sail on 1 April 1900 from Hamburg to Portland, Oregon, under Captain James McMurty. After docking off the American coast she sailed successively to Durban, South Africa, then Newcastle, New South Wales, and Caleta Buena, in South America. In the course of these journeys the ship picked up two new crew members, Victor Baileff, a native of Jersey and a cook by profession, in Durban, and Valeri Giovanni, an Italian, in New South Wales. Giovanni was the only Italian on board ship, and could not speak a word of English. Perhaps for this reason, Baileff took to teasing him regularly. Other members of the crew joined in, but the Jersey cook was apparently the ringleader.

Matters came to a head when the ship docked in Caleta Buena, and both men took each other on in a bare-knuckle fight. Giovanni was soundly beaten, and swore he would get even at the first opportunity. On 7 December 1900 the ship set sail for Falmouth, with a cargo of nitrates. The vanquished man bided his time, until on 8 February when he went to McMurty to complain – through an apprentice, Thomas Rooney, who spoke fluent Italian – about the teasing he claimed he was continually getting from Baileff and some of the other crew members. The captain told him to 'go forward', and promised he would personally intervene to 'put it right' if it happened again. As Giovanni did not raise the matter a second time, it was assumed that matters had improved.

One week later, at about 5.30 a.m. on 15 February, the second mate, Robert Garnett, sent Giovanni and Baileff to wash down the deck. About an hour later he sent Baileff down the forehatch to repair a sail, while Giovanni was told to clean out one of the lifeboats. As he went to the forecastle hold for a bucket and brush, the latter seized his chance. He went down to the galley and asked for a drink of water.

While Baileff had his back turned, the Italian took a knife and walked out quietly carrying it in his pocket. Moments later Garnett heard a cry, and went down the forehatch to find Baileff lying on his back in a bending position, with Giovanni holding a knife over him in his right hand, and his left arm round the victim's back. Garnett saw Giovanni raise the knife and plunge it into Baileff's heart. He shouted out for someone to fetch the captain, as Giovanni dropped the knife and made a half-hearted attempt to run away from them between the decks. As he had no realistic chance of getting away, he soon gave himself up.

Garnett opened Baileff's shirt, and saw several stab wounds. Death had been more or less instantaneous, but after his body was examined it was seen that the Italian was so bent on revenge that he inflicted eight wounds on his victim. When Baileff was buried at sea, Rooney turned to Giovanni and said to him in Italian, 'See what you have done.' 'Throw it overboard,' Giovanni retorted. 'I don't wish to see it any more.' 'Why did you kill him with the knife?' Rooney asked. 'Revenge for Caleta Buena', was the answer.

Giovanni was kept in irons until the ship docked at Falmouth in April, and then taken into custody. The case was tried at Bodmin Assizes on 17 June under Mr Justice Wills, with Mr Fraser Macleod and Mr J.R. Randolph for the prosecution, and Mr W.T. Lawrance for the defence. At first the prisoner pleaded guilty, though on the advice of his counsel, he then withdrew that plea and entered one of not guilty.

After hearing evidence from those involved on board ship, Lawrance argued that the jury should return a verdict not of wilful murder, but 'of lesser gravity'. The prisoner, he said, had been terrified of taunts from the rest of the crew. While much of the teasing may have been meant as harmless banter, Giovanni claimed that it had included sinister threats on Baileff's part, including one to put him in a bag and throw him overboard. The Italians 'were a highly sensitive race, quick to imagine an affront, quick to resent it, and quick to exaggerate the sense of personal danger'.

Macleod argued that it would require acts of the very gravest provocation to reduce a crime from murder to manslaughter, and there had been no suggestion of any acts or deeds on the part of the deceased. His unprovoked death at the hands of Giovanni was nothing but a cold-blooded and vengeful murder.

In summing up the judge reminded the jury of the number and position of stabs that had been inflicted on Baileff. It had been such a vicious assault that it was difficult to suppose a man could inflict such injuries on another without intending to kill him.

The jury returned a verdict of wilful murder, with a recommendation to mercy. When Giovanni was informed through an interpreter and asked if he had anything to say as to why sentence should not be passed, he said nothing. While in the cells awaiting his ultimate fate, he was visited by the Revd Father Smith, and confessed to his crime. On 7 July 1901, he was hanged by James and William Billington. Aged thirty-one, he was the first man to die on the gallows of Bodmin Gaol for nineteen years.

12

'I SUPPOSE IT WAS TEMPER'

St Erth, 1909

In the early years of the twentieth century there was often more opportunity for miners to work abroad than at home. One young man who discovered this for himself was William Hampton, of St Erth, who spent a year or so working in the United States. Yet the pull of home remained strong, and in November 1907, at the age of twenty-one, he returned to his home town. Early the following year he became engaged to Emily Barnes Trewarthen Tredrea, who lived in a cottage nearby in New Row, Old Vicarage Gate. She too came from a mining family. Her father John also spent long periods away from home as he had found work in the mines at Johannesburg, and she shared the cottage with her mother Grace, and her three younger siblings.

In the spring of 1908 Hampton moved into the Tredreas' cottage as a lodger. Towards the end of the year, he said that he was expecting to go to work in America again, but would not stay there long. By the time he returned, they would have enough money to marry and settle down together in a home of their own at or near St Erth.

Emily was a bright, cheerful girl of fifteen, and the neighbours said she always seemed to be singing. However the course of true love did not run smoothly in this case. Grace Tredrea had known William since he was a boy, and thought he would make her daughter an excellent husband, but after a while Emily had second thoughts. She was increasingly irritated by his uncouth manners and persistent swearing; at length she realised she no longer cared for him, to the extent of telling one of her friends in the village that she hated him, was afraid of him, and feared he might kill her. On Saturday 1 May 1909, she told him it was all over between them and she wanted to break off the engagement.

At first he did not react, and he probably assumed she would reconsider. It was equally probable that Grace Tredrea's presence in the house acted as some kind of restraint on his behaviour. This was not the case on Sunday night, when Grace had to go out at about 10 p.m. to look in on her elderly mother, who suffered from a bad leg and needed to be kept a regular eye on. Unaware of any problems between the young couple, she was happy to leave them in the house. Also at the house were William, her nine-year-old brother, her sister of five, and the fifteen-month-old baby. The latter started to cry as Mrs Tredrea was about to leave, so

St Erth. (© Nicola Sly)

she was brought downstairs and Emily held her in her arms, trying to settle her. Sometime after she had put her little sister down another conversation ensued, and Emily told William Hampton that she had not changed her mind. She did not want to have anything more to do with him. At this he lost his temper, grabbed her, threw her on the floor and pressed his hands tightly around her throat.

William had been upstairs in bed, asleep. He was woken by what he later described as 'a kind of rattling noise', and got out of bed, partly dressed, then went downstairs to see what was going on. He saw Hampton with his sister on the floor, his knee on her body, keeping her down, with his thumbs around her throat, choking her. His first instinct was to go and fetch their mother, and tried to leave the house. Hampton would not let him go; 'Step back, I am going out in a minute, and you can go out with me.' William asked what the matter was with his sister, and Hampton said she was very sick. The boy insisted that he wanted to go into the garden. Aware that it would make no difference to his ultimate fate, Hampton allowed him to go.

Before William left the house, he saw Hampton lift Emily up and try to make her stand in the corner of the room. As she was almost certainly dead by this time, there was no point, so he then placed her in a chair, her head falling limply to one side. William went as quickly as he could in the direction of his grandmother's house. He had only gone a few yards when he heard the door bang, and as he looked back he saw Hampton leaping over the hedge near the house and running off in the direction of Hayle.

Grace Tredrea soon came home, followed immediately by PC Ashford, who had been alerted to the problem. On arrival they found Emily's body still in the chair where Hampton had placed her. The baby was in another armchair, and it was assumed that Emily had put her there while she went to get a cup of tea and some biscuits. Between them, Ashford, Frank Trevaskis, the local postmaster and his brother carried the body upstairs and attempted artificial respiration, but it was too late. Ashford then started to search for Hampton. They checked the house, garden and outhouses, but there was no sign of him.

News travelled fast, and already several of the neighbours were aware that trouble had been brewing. Ashford enlisted the services of several young men with bicycles, who went to Hayle, Levant, and other villages in the district to tell the policemen what had occurred, and to ask them to join him at St Erth where their presence was needed. Another local resident, Cardell Williams, came and offered to give Emily artificial respiration again, though it was too late. Two policemen soon arrived, as did Dr Davis, who made a thorough examination of the body. He found very severe injuries to the throat; such had been the pressure of Hampton's hands that the skin was torn, and there was a small bruise on the left temple, which might have been caused by a blow sustained in a struggle.

By now the police had obtained a full description of Hampton. Sergeant Kent organised a search party, and there was no shortage of volunteers to help. They called at his father's cottage, searched in several outhouses, and even checked a deep pit near the church in case he had jumped in. However Hampton was aware that there would be no hiding place for him, and he surrendered to the inevitable. After running out of the house, he went across the fields to Foundry, Hayle, and then to Copperhouse. After some hesitation, at around midnight he met two constables near the police station.

'Have you heard the news?' he asked them, and then added, 'I might as well give myself up.' When they asked him what news he was referring to, he said, 'I think I have killed a maid at St Erth.' PC Roberts questioned him further, and asked Hampton how he did it. 'I choked her,' he told him. After a few more questions, Roberts said it was 'rather a funny story' (one assumes he meant funny in the odd sense), and suggested that perhaps the girl was not dead. Hampton was more positive; 'I think she is dead right enough, because I picked her up and she could not stand, and then I put her in a chair and her head fell over one side, meat came out of her mouth, and her lips were black.'

Why did he do such a thing, the policeman asked. 'I was going with her, and now she won't have anything to do with me. I suppose it was temper that caused me to do it.' Roberts took him into custody, and then went to St Erth to tell Sergeant Kent that the search could be called off. All his helpers were relieved, as many had sworn they would not go to bed that night unless they heard that the killer had been captured.

Pleading not guilty to a charge of 'wilful murder', Hampton went on trial at Bodmin on 24 June 1909 under Mr Justice Phillimore, with Mr Raymond Asquith and Mr Stafford Howard prosecuting, and Mr R.G. Seton defending.

The first witness to be called was Grace Tredrea. She said she had never known her daughter and the prisoner to quarrel, but knew her daughter objected to his swearing. On the Friday or Saturday before the crime, she heard Emily tell him, 'I don't think I shall go with you any more.' Even so, she had no idea of any impending tragedy, until young William came to look for her after Hampton had strangled Emily. Mother and son hurried home, meeting Constable Ashford on the way, and found the lifeless Emily in a wicker chair.

When questioned about her daughter's personality, Mrs Tredrea said that the girl was 'most industrious and respectable', and not nervous by nature, 'but

Bodmin Gaol. Built in 1777, the gaol witnessed fifty-five hangings, the last being that of William Hampton in July 1909. Closed in 1922, it now contains a museum and licensed restaurant open to the public. (© Kim Van der Kiste)

sometimes fainted when she had nervous attacks'. She had never known the prisoner give the police any trouble before. William then followed his mother into the witness box and described the events of that fatal night as he had seen them. The policemen involved, then Dr Davis, all followed him in giving their evidence. Also for the prosecution, Mr Asquith said there was no doubt that the prisoner killed the deceased by strangling her. The girl's brother had given his evidence with remarkable accuracy for a child of his age. There was nothing to suggest that the prisoner had been provoked, and he showed no remorse for his crime, making no efforts to revive the girl or get assistance after he had attacked her. His murder was the result of a grudge, a feeling of resentment, 'a premeditated crime' in which he was determined to wreak vengeance at the first opportunity, 'a cold-blooded crime, carried out with ferocity.'

For the defence, Mr Seton said there was no doubt that the person who caused the death of the girl was the prisoner, but it was a question of provocation, not of malice. The verdict should be one of manslaughter. If the intention was murder, as the prosecution averred, and the prisoner seriously meant to commit the worst possible crime, there had been ample means for him to use one of the knives lying on the kitchen table. In this case there was every reason why the verdict of the jury should be that of manslaughter.

In summing up the judge said that the jury were asked by Mr Seton to say it was not murder. 'Provocation was not a plea they could give much heed to.' The act had not been a momentary one, and all the evidence suggested that the prisoner had intended for some time to take the life of the deceased.

The jury were out for fifteen minutes before delivering a verdict of guilty, but with a recommendation to mercy. The judge told him that this would be 'forwarded to the proper quarter, but I advise you to prepare for your death.' Hampton stood calmly in the dock, showing no emotion, and did not reply when asked if he had anything to say as to why sentence of death should not be passed on him. When he was led out to the gallows on 20 July to be hanged by Henry and Thomas Pierrepoint, he became the last person ever to be executed at Bodmin Gaol.

13

'I BELIEVE I HAVE DONE IT'

Kingsand, 1910

At fifty-five Surgeon-Major James Hamilton Nicholas had had a distinguished career in the Royal Army Medical Corps which took him overseas to India, Burma and Africa among other places. After this he was looking forward to retirement at Southfields, Croydon, where he lived with his wife and children. Before he gave up working completely he maintained a small but select private practice, and a brass plate affixed to the railings advertised the fact.

Ironically, the surgeon's family life had for some time been blighted by the ill-health of his son, also called James Hamilton Nicholas. Born in 1884, James the younger suffered from a heart condition and had been operated on for appendicitis, and his parents were extremely protective of him. To add to this, he had more recently had mental problems. In 1903 he emigrated to New Zealand, living and working on a ranch. He wrote home regularly, and the family gathered that far from being happy, he was leading 'a rough and solitary sort of life'. In April 1909 he had sunstroke, followed by a bout of fever and religious melancholia. His desperately worried father went out in August to see him and bring him home, but the young man was too ill to return. As he had shown signs of insanity, he was admitted to an asylum at Auckland for a while.

In January 1910 his father went to New Zealand a second time to fetch him. After he had faithfully promised the medical authorities that the family were capable of looking after him, they came back to England on 20 May. The younger James was still not fully recovered, and during the whole of their journey on board ship he had a keeper who could supervise him all the time.

During the next few weeks it was clear that he still had a long way to go. The family, which included his sister Yvonne as well as his parents, could not allow him to go out by himself, and two of them had to be with him all the time in order to restrain him should he become violent. They were advised to lock him in at night, and had wooden shutters fixed to his windows, to stop him from wandering off. He chafed at being watched all the time, and though he would not say anything, he always had a haunted, worried look.

On 28 July 1910 they moved from Croydon to Cornwall, where they settled into a new home, Cliff House, at Kingsand, on the southern coast and close to the border with Devon. At first the change of scene seemed to do him good.

Kingsand and Cawsand, c. 1920.

During their first week at Cliff House he seemed better and brighter, but after that he went back to his old ways. He had fits of sudden temper when thwarted, and when told to do things by his father, he turned his back and said he was 'not going to put up with that sort of thing any longer'. He particularly resented not being allowed to bathe at Kingsand because of his weak heart, and after he had defied orders and bathed one weekend there was a family row which left the younger James with a feeling of bitter resentment. In addition he was only allowed to smoke at certain times, and not eat between meals.

Poor James, the family thought, had been insane since his return to England. They were all frightened of him, and feared it might end in tragedy. Mrs Nicholas continually begged her husband to get a keeper for the young man. There was a history of mental instability in the family, and her own brother had needed a keeper at home. When a keeper at Auckland Asylum who had seen the younger James returned to England, Mrs Nicholas was ready to employ him, and prepared a bed for him in the house. As a former surgeon in the RAMC, Major Nicholas was most offended at any suggestion that he might not be able to control his own son; he was not afraid of the young man, and refused to hear of the idea. Yvonne and her mother were so afraid of their brother that whenever they took him for a walk at Croydon, they always went where there were tramlines or police, so that if anything terrible happened they would be in a position to summon help immediately.

On 15 August Mrs Nicholas warned her husband that she feared their son was turning against him, and that either he ought to have a keeper, or would have to be sent away. Once more the Major dismissed any such idea. He would not live long to regret doing so. That evening all the family went for a walk to Anderton. It was fine well into the evening, and they returned home soon after 9.30 p.m. The younger James went to bed as usual in the room adjoining that of his parents.

At 3 a.m. the next morning, Yvonne was woken by the sound of someone falling downstairs, followed by a second sound, as if somebody had dropped to the floor. She opened her bedroom door and saw her brother going downstairs, then heard her father call out 'Bring a light', and her mother say 'Coming'. Yvonne asked what was going on, and her mother told her to come downstairs. As it was still dark upstairs she crept down carefully to the drawing room to investigate, and saw the faint light of a candle. This revealed the sight of Major Nicholas lying on the floor, his son kneeling beside him, and her mother trying to pull the latter away. Then the candle went out, and her mother called a servant.

At that point Yvonne saw her brother fumbling with her father's throat, though he looked as if he did not know what he was doing. He did not seem at all angry or excited. After their mother left the room, Yvonne realised that her brother appeared to be trying to throttle their father. She tried to pull him off, but he shouted out, 'Let go.' In a little while his arm relaxed, and when she pulled it away she saw to her horror that in his hand he had an enamelled knife, which she took away from him. There was a collection of several similar weapons hanging on the drawing room wall. As he relinquished his grip on his father's throat, he said, 'That is done! That is done!' Their mother and a servant then came in, and their mother told James to go back to his room. He went up to bed, looking dazed, as though he was dreaming.

At 5.40 a.m. Mrs Nicholas telephoned Dr J. Trelawney Cheves, who arrived at the house within the hour. He went upstairs to the drawing room, and the first thing he saw was a candlestick lying on the floor. There was an occasional table on its side, both objects evidently having been knocked over in the struggle. Just beside the archway which divided the room he saw the body of Major Nicholas, dressed in his pyjamas, lying flat on his back, his legs stretched out, and his fists clenched. There was a small amount of blood on the front of his pyjamas, and two pools of coagulated blood behind the head, suggesting that there had not been a struggle. In addition there was a long horizontal wound on the chin, and a deep gash in the throat. A vacant space could be seen in the display of knives in a recess on the wall. The doctor concluded that the major had been knocked down by a blow on the chin which rendered him unconscious, and then the attacker cut his throat. He had sustained both wounds when he was lying down, and neither could possibly have been self-inflicted.

The police at Kingsand were contacted at once, and PC Mitchell came to arrest James Nicholas. When Mitchell went to the bedroom the door was open about five inches, and he could see James Nicholas on the other side. 'Hello Ham, what is the matter?' he called out. To his surprise 'Ham' did not appear in an agitated condition, and seemed very calm and quiet. When the policeman spoke to him he laughed, 'I believe I have done it.' On being cautioned and charged with the murder of his father, he admitted a second time, 'Yes, I did it.'

An inquest was held the following day, 17 August, at Kingsand. Mr A. Glubb, the District Coroner at Liskeard, was a close relative of the family and though present in court, took no part in the proceedings which were conducted by his deputy, Mr A. Venning, with Mr E. Elliot Square appearing for the relatives. After hearing evidence from Yvonne Nicholas, Superintendent Gard of Liskeard, PC Mitchell of Kingsand and Inspector Roberts of Torpoint on behalf of the

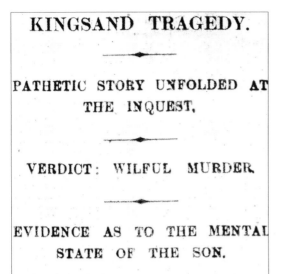

KINGSAND TRAGEDY.

PATHETIC STORY UNFOLDED AT THE INQUEST.

VERDICT: WILFUL MURDER

EVIDENCE AS TO THE MENTAL STATE OF THE SON.

Detail from the Western Morning News, *18 August 1910, reporting on the inquest into Major James Nicholas.*

police, and Dr Cheves, Mr Venning said that the question of the prisoner's mental condition would be considered at another court. Mitchell confirmed that he did not show any signs of violence while in his bedroom before or after arrest. The weapon was produced in court, and a juror told them that it was a Gurkha knife, part of a collection mounted in a drawing room by a previous owner of Cliff House. None of the knives were sheathed.

In returning a verdict of 'Wilful murder', the foreman of the jury expressed their deepest sympathy with the widow and family.

On 21 October James Nicholas, who was described as a medical student, was charged before Mr Justice Bankes at Bodmin Assizes with murdering his father. Mr Hawke was conducting the defence, instructed by Mr Elliot Square, while Mr Emmanuel led the counsel for the prosecution, though in the end the latter's services were not required.

Dr Wolferstan, medical officer at Mutley Prison, Plymouth, said that Nicholas had been under his care since 16 August, the day he had killed his father. He was clearly of unsound mind, had delusions that he was occasionally visited by spirits, and was suffering from impulsive insanity. He had a very defective memory, could not fix his mind or any subject for more than a very limited period, and would therefore be unable to instruct his counsel on any points that might arise in the case. He had indicated his insanity while in prison, and on the previous night he had tried to attack the officer in charge.

Mr Hawke had other witnesses whom he proposed to call, but the judge said this would not be necessary. He then addressed the jury, saying that this procedure was rather unusual. The prisoner was charged with murder, and the policy of the law was that no man should be convicted of a crime if members of the jury were satisfied that at the time he committed it, 'he was insane in the sense in which the law had described it.' But the law went further, and said it was not right that any man should be put upon trial unless his mind was in such a state as to enable him to comprehend exactly what was going on. They must be satisfied that the man was insane in the sense that he could not fully appreciate what was going on and keep his attention fixed on all the evidence given against him. If they were of that opinion, they ought to return a verdict that he was of unsound mind and unable to plead.

It was more or less a foregone conclusion. Poor, mentally unstable James Nicholas was no cold-blooded murderer, and the judge ordered him to be detained during His Majesty's Pleasure.

14

'ALL THAT A MAN COULD WISH FOR'

Skinner's Bottom, 1920

On the morning of Sunday 25 January 1920 Jack Pryor paid a visit to his old friend, farmer and cattle dealer Joseph Charles Hoare. The latter and his housekeeper Laura Sara kept a dilapidated smallholding in the hamlet of Skinner's Bottom, just outside Redruth. Pryor approached the run-down cottage and as usual called out a greeting, but for once there came no reply. Puzzled, he looked over the garden wall and saw the housekeeper, barefoot and still dressed in her nightclothes, lying battered and bloody by the cottage door.

Pryor immediately rushed to the house next door to rouse the neighbours, the Tonkin family, who sent for the police. When he went back to Hoare's cottage, in the company of Constable Stephens from nearby Blackwater, the injured woman was struggling vainly to get up from the ground. To their horror, they then spotted Hoare lying by the garden gate. He was bleeding severely from the head, trying desperately to staunch his wounds with a piece of old sacking. Both Hoare and his housekeeper were barely alive. The policemen sent Pryor to summon the doctor from Chacewater, then carried the victims into the cottage, and administered first aid. Hoare's wounds were more severe and he survived for only five minutes, while Sara clung to life for almost two hours. By the time Dr Forsyth arrived, both were dead and all he could do was to carry out a brief examination of the bodies to try and determine the cause of death. He noted that they had died from severe head injuries, as a result of being struck with a blunt object which fractured their skulls. The weapon was a stout, knobbly tree branch, weighing about 4lb, discovered in the garden about 20ft from where Hoare had lain.

It had been assumed that Laura Sara was Hoare's housekeeper, but there was evidence of a more intimate relationship between them. When police searched the rundown, somewhat isolated cottage where they lived, they noticed an unmade bed that must have been recently occupied by two people. Sara, aged forty at the time of her death, was married to but separated from her husband, Hugh, for more than twenty years. She had borne six children, all but one of whom had subsequently died.

Sara was known to have a hot temper and had, on one occasion, hit her own mother over the head with a large stick. She was inclined to drink to excess and, shortly after leaving her husband, had been convicted of assisting in keeping a disorderly house in Truro.

Hoare, aged fifty-seven, was known to associate with women of easy virtue, and it was Sara's liberal dispensation of sexual favours that had led to them moving in together, first in Truro, then in the sleepy hamlet of Skinner's Bottom. They seemed happy together; Hoare apparently loved and cared for Sara, to the extent that he had recently made a will in her favour. In spite of her drinking and fiery temper, he obviously trusted her, describing her as 'all that a man could wish for.'

However, despite their outward appearance as a happily domesticated couple, Sara enjoyed the company of other men, and local gossip suggested that she was taking advantage of Hoare's feelings for her. After the murders, there were rumours that one of Sara's gentlemen friends – or even perhaps her ex-husband – may have wanted to gain possession of Hoare's estate. Indeed, with Hoare dead, had she survived him, Sara stood to inherit his smallholding, stock and an additional sum of £200 from his bank accounts.

Police searched the small cottage and spoke to neighbours in an effort to gain some insight into the sequence of events leading to the couple's violent demise. The cottage lights had been off at around 10 p.m. on the night before the murders and neighbours assumed that the couple had retired for the night. One neighbour had heard Hoare's dog barking at around 7.15 a.m. on the morning of the killings, but did not think it sufficiently unusual to investigate.

The wood used to inflict the horrific head injuries on the couple appeared to have been taken from a log pile, situated next to a cowshed at the rear of the cottage. A significant amount of blood was found on and around the cowshed, suggesting that a violent struggle had taken place there, before Hoare had managed to stagger to the spot near the gate where he was ultimately found.

The police tried to establish who might have killed the couple and why. One theory that arose was that Hoare and Sara had argued and had come to blows, each being responsible for inflicting wounds on the other. However the fact that only one bloodstained weapon was found seemed to discount this theory. It was thought more likely that someone had lain in wait for Hoare, taking him by surprise and attacking him as he went about his normal Sunday routine. The noise of the attack could have brought Sara from the house to investigate, and, if she had recognised the attacker, she could easily have been killed to prevent her from identifying him.

If this was the case, what had been the motive for the attacks? Hoare was generally well-liked and known as an easy-going man, although with a fondness for drink on occasion. Admittedly he was relatively well off, but the majority of his money was kept securely in a bank account. He was known to secrete money in various places around his house, and also to carry cash about his person in a little cloth bag in his waistcoat. Yet when the bodies were found, the empty bag was safely buttoned closed and large sums of money in the cottage remained undisturbed. This left police wondering if the killer had been someone with a personal grudge against Hoare.

An inquest was opened during which the coroner addressed the jury, outlining three possible scenarios. The first of these was murder/suicide – one party had struck and killed the other, then committed suicide. Alternatively both parties had struggled together resulting in the deaths of both. Or could the blows to both have been struck by a third person?

Cornish police and experts from Scotland Yard at the Hoare and Sara murder site, January 1920. (Royal Cornwall Museum, Truro)

Given that beating oneself repeatedly over the head with a branch is an unlikely means of committing suicide and that only one weapon was found, the first two theories hardly seemed to hold water. Besides, the man who had carried out the post-mortem examinations, Dr Forsyth, effectively discounted both based on the evidence of his examination of the bodies.

Forsyth maintained that Hoare had been struck a single, traverse blow to the head, the blow fracturing the frontal bone of his skull into five pieces. Whereas he agreed that Laura Sara had sufficient physical strength to render such a blow, he thought it unlikely that she could have done so after being injured herself. And he believed that, given the severity of his own injuries, it would not have been possible for Hoare to strike and kill Sara after being wounded himself, particularly as she was found to have an unusually thick skull.

The inquest was adjourned while the police continued their enquiries and tried to establish the identity of the mysterious third person. A decision was made to call in reinforcements from Scotland Yard, but still it seemed impossible to throw any more light on the violent and bloody deaths of Hoare and his housekeeper. Thus, when the coroner's inquiry resumed, police were no further forward in their search for suspects.

At the inquiry, both Pryor and Tonkin were severely rebuked by the coroner for not rendering first aid to the dying housekeeper and for waiting for the arrival of the police constable before making any attempt to help. It was then left to Chief Inspector Heldon of Scotland Yard to address the jury. He admitted that he had dismissed all rumours surrounding the case. Robbery seemed unlikely since substantial amounts of cash remained undisturbed in the cottage, and nobody had been seen lying in wait near the house. He also disagreed with jealousy as the motive for the killings, since there was no concrete evidence to support the theory.

Then, in the absence of any physical evidence, a clear motive and any viable suspects, he outlined his own personal theory as to the course of events. He concluded that Hoare and Sara had effectively murdered each other, with Sara striking the first blow. He intimated that Sara had led a somewhat wild life and may have felt dissatisfied, confined in a rather dilapidated cottage in a tiny hamlet where there was precious little excitement to be had. She was aware that Hoare had named her beneficiary of his will and had thought to speed up her inheritance by violent means. Sara, said Heldon, had decided to slip downstairs and murder Hoare, before returning to her bed where she could later claim to have been sleeping soundly when the body was found.

However, the presence of bloodstains proved that Hoare had not been poleaxed by the blow, but instead had been sufficiently conscious to stagger the few yards from the cowshed to the garden gate before collapsing. Heldon had carried out some experiments at the scene of the crime. He found that, if he aimed blows at an imaginary person standing in the exact spot where the housekeeper was assumed to have fallen, the stick was inclined to fly from his hands, landing remarkably close to where it had been discovered on the day of the murders. Thus, he theorised, Hoare had been first struck by Sara, but had managed to wrest the branch from her grasp. He had hit her a couple of times before swinging the branch and missing, causing it to shoot out of his hands.

Yet Heldon's solution to the mystery was not without its critics. It emerged that several reliable witnesses had seen Hoare and Sara drinking in the Red Lion Inn at Blackwater with a stranger on the night before the murders. Throughout the evening Hoare was free with his money, making it quite plain to anyone watching that he was a man of considerable means and possibly setting himself up as a potential target for robbery. After leaving the pub, the three were seen riding together in a horse and cart, heading towards Skinner's Bottom. Inside the house, a telegram was found that appeared to have been sent by Hoare and Sara, inviting the recipient to come and stay with them. It was never established to whom the telegram was sent. It appears that all the evidence – the mysterious stranger in the pub, the telegram and the wounds to both victims – pointed to the presence of a third person. Was Heldon so keen to solve the puzzle that he elected to ignore this evidence, opting instead to implicate Sara so that the case might be closed as quickly as possible?

The verdict of the jury hinged on whom they found to be most believable, Chief Inspector Heldon or Dr Forsyth. They deliberated for less than thirty minutes before accepting Forsyth's version of events, returning their verdict of wilful murder by person or persons unknown.

As a result the identity of the murderer(s) of Joseph Hoare and his housekeeper Laura Sara, if indeed there was a murderer, remains unknown. To this day nobody has ever been charged with the killings.

15

'NEVER HAD POISON OF ANY KIND'

Edward Ernest Black was born in Burnley in 1886. At the age of twenty-one the family moved to Tregonissey, where he, his father and two brothers were employed in the local china clay works, though father and brothers later returned to Lancashire. For a while he lived with Annie Nicholls, a native of Duloe who had lived in Tregonissey since childhood. Fifteen years his senior, with a small daughter, Marion, from a previous relationship, she was a teacher at Carclaze School for some years and then took over running the village general store adjoining their house at Lane End, Tregonissey. In 1914 Edward and Annie were married. He was rejected for military service on health grounds, possibly as the result of an industrial accident, and after he left the china clay works he took a post as an insurance agent for the Refuge Assurance Company. He had a fine bass voice as a singer and in his spare time he sang with the St Austell Church Choir. He was also a member of the local Red Cross detachment, and regularly attended football matches at the St Austell ground to assist with first aid.

To the local community, Edward Black was a fine upstanding citizen, always ready to play an active role in the area. Nevertheless some saw a very different side of him. As an insurance agent he was either very unlucky and unsuccessful, or else totally unscrupulous – probably the latter. Several of his customers paid good money for the delivery of policies which were later proved to be non-existent. By the time they realised, he had spent the proceeds, and on 2 November 1921 his employers dismissed him.

During the previous month, on 21 October, Annie had complained of feeling unwell. Nine days later she, her husband and daughter went for a walk together, during which she told them she had been feeling poorly that week. At breakfast on 31 October her husband poured tea out for the three of them from a teapot on the hearth. About an hour later Annie began vomiting severely and complaining of pains in her side. Edward called Dr Andrew, who did not consider the trouble serious and assumed it was probably ordinary gastritis. However Annie's condition may have given her husband an idea with regard to settling his debts. Eight days later he purchased two ounces of arsenic from the local branch of Timothy White's, the chemist, and signed the poisons register. During the next few days Annie became worse, and complained that the medicine burned like pepper in her throat every time it was administered by her husband. Dr Andrew began to have his suspicions.

On 8 November Black said he was going to cycle to St Austell to get some cigarettes for Annie's shop. He left her in the care of his stepdaughter Marion, now aged sixteen, and the neighbours, particularly Ann Best, one of Annie's closest friends, who had helped to nurse her.

Annie never saw him again. She had a relapse on 10 November, was violently sick and in severe pain. During the night she became weaker and died at 1 a.m. the next morning. Suspecting something more than natural causes, Dr Andrew refused to issue a certificate of death, but informed the police, and passed stomach samples to the pathologist Dr Bernard Spilsbury for analysis. A post-mortem was opened at St Austell three days later by the Coroner, Mr M. Edyvean, and adjourned pending arrival of the Home Office analyst's report on the contents of her stomach, which Police Inspector Trythall stated was expected within a week. (It was delayed and the inquest was not resumed until the next month). The only witness present was Miss Nicholls, who was asked by the coroner to confirm her identity, and that she, her mother and stepfather all lived at the same address. The jury were offered a chance to ask her any further questions but the foreman, ex-Police Inspector Hugo, assured Mr Edyvean that she was well-known to them all. This, said the coroner, was all the evidence he needed at this stage.

That same day, police questioning led to further information about Black's recent movements. After he had gone to St Austell, apparently for more cigarettes, he left his bicycle in the yard of a temperance house in the town, and caught the 6 p.m. train to Plymouth. One of his business associates confirmed seeing him at the station, and Black told him that he was going to Par, but would return later that evening. Black did not keep the appointment, and when questioned none of his friends had any idea where he had gone.

At this stage only a few people were aware that cases relating to his malpractice were about to come to court, and that he could probably not afford to reimburse the victims of his little frauds. His father had recently died, though his mother and brothers were still living in Burnley; he also had relatives at Cowdenbeath, Fife, and it was thought that after leaving Plymouth he might have gone north to either of these places.

Further extensive police enquiries revealed that a man answering his description had left St Austell wearing a grey suit with a grey trilby hat and dark tan lace-up boots, was later seen at Burnley in a dark suit and light cap, and had changed his brown boots for black ones. When the police tried to trace his movements, they had good reason to believe that he had been in Plymouth briefly on 9 November, and secured a sum of £50 from a local firm with whom he had regularly done business in the past. When he called upon them he told a plausible story about not having enough money with him to complete the purchase of some furniture he had come to Plymouth to buy, and if he wired home for the money it could not arrive before his train left Plymouth for St Austell. The people he spoke to had no reason not to trust him, and a very contented Black left the building with the money in his pocket. A fellow insurance agent in George Street reported having seen him on the next morning, after which it was assumed that he left Millbay Station on the 10.25 a.m. train, and arrived in Manchester at 7.30 p.m. in the evening. Part of the money he borrowed must have gone on new clothing, but it would take more than a change of apparel to remain beyond the long arm of the law.

On 15 November Mrs Black's funeral was held. The Revd T.S. Lea officiated, and several villagers accompanied the cortège from the house to the St Austell cemetery. The principal mourner was Marion, whom the press described as 'a pathetic figure (who) exhibited acute distress, particularly at the graveside', where she was supported by Mr Bertrand Parnell, superintendent of the Refuge Insurance Company. Few, if any knew, that she had an extra cross to bear, as well as the sudden death of her mother. Not long before, she had learnt that she was not her mother's adopted daughter, something she had always assumed, but a child born out of wedlock.

A committee was spontaneously formed by the villagers, with Mr Parnell as one of the trustees, to help provide financially for Marion and enable her to continue the studies she had recently begun to follow in her mother's footsteps as a schoolteacher. After consideration she decided that she would leave her studies and continue working at the family shop. Shortly before her death Annie Black had made a will, leaving the furniture to her daughter, who decided she would retain the piano, music stool and a few other small mementoes, but wished to sell most of it by auction. She would keep the shop as a back-up establishment, and live with her neighbour, Mrs Kent, so they could let the rest of the house.

That same day the police took possession of a number of bottles, photographs and papers found at the Blacks' house. One item, which was only to be expected in view of his activities within the community, was a first aid book. However, this particular copy was folded down at the section dealing with arsenic poisoning. It would form a small but significant part of the evidence for the prosecution.

Also on 15 November a warrant was issued for the arrest of Black on two charges of obtaining money under false pretences, after both cases involving Black's malpractice were heard at St Austell County Court. In the first, Miss Norah Smith of Foxhole sued him for delivery of a policy in the Refuge Assurance Company, or another insurance company, on the life of John Rowse, to the value of £50. Alternatively she would claim £50 damages for non-delivery of the policy, as in February 1921 she had lent the defendant £15 on the security of a policy said to exist in the Refuge Company, and later gave him another £15, but never received the policy. Her solicitor said the company did not exist, and judgment was given for the plaintiff. In the second, Charles Smith, also of Foxhole, brought an action against Black for dissolution of the partnership said to exist between the parties in regard to certain Cunard shares and an account of the partnership dealings, assets, and liabilities. Again, it was clear that Black had obtained money by false pretences, and judgement was given for Smith.

On 19 November St Austell and Fowey played a charity cup football match on the former's home ground, and a first aider was required on the pitch several times. Whenever he appeared, there were shouts from the crowd of 'Where's Black?' The community could talk of little else that week, and the regular question 'Have they found him yet?' could only mean one thing.

While his whereabouts remained uncertain, the police took the precaution of contacting liners which had sailed the previous day. It was thought that he might have tried to leave Plymouth by liner, especially since he had visited the town a couple of times recently, without the knowledge of his wife or stepdaughter. He would have been unable to book a passage on such a vessel because of the inevitable passport problems he would face, but there was always the possibility that he might have left England as a member of a ship's crew. Those who knew him thought he was most unlikely to have committed suicide.

On Monday 21 November Joseph James Kelly, a Tregonissey butcher and one of Marion's guardians, received a letter from Black, with the address simply given as 'Burnley' and posted at Southport on the previous Friday or Saturday. It mentioned the names of several other people who had cooperated with the recipient in arranging Black's home affairs, and asked for the letter expressing his thanks to be shown them. Referring to the charges alleged against him, he protested that although he had made the greatest mistake of his life in leaving home under the circumstances, he was innocent and had nothing to do with his wife's death. It added that by the time this letter arrived, he would be 'hundreds of miles away' and that he would not be brought back to St Austell alive. Kelly promptly handed this letter to the police, who thought that if it had been posted at the weekend, Black must have been lying low in Lancashire all week. If he was still in England, his early arrest would be inevitable, but if he had gone to Ireland, his chances of escape were greater.

As Liverpool was the main English port in the area, and therefore the place from which he would be likely to effect an escape, efforts were concentrated on the area. Descriptions and photographs of him were published in the regional newspapers. He was 5ft 7in tall, readers were told, had black hair, was clean-shaven, with a heart tattooed on his left wrist and had a slight curvature of the spine which caused a lean to his left as he walked. It was not noticeable when he was standing erect or sitting upright, but only when stooping.

On the evening of 21 November a Mr Stevens, claiming to be a commercial traveller from Preston, booked in at Cashin's Temperance Hotel in Bell Street, Liverpool. Fortuitously, it was within a stone's throw of the Liverpool Central Police Station in Dale Street. When he presented himself at the reception desk the proprietress, described by the press as 'a youngish widow of smart appearance and great intelligence', whose name was deliberately not disclosed for obvious reasons, was unaware of the hue and cry going on.

As business was fairly quiet, she had a friendly conversation with him, just as she often had with other guests when there was time. He immediately struck her as being very genial and friendly. For about an hour, she later told the police, 'we talked on a variety of subjects. During the conversation he did not say much about himself, other than that he had been travelling about considerably, and among other places which he had visited he mentioned Hull and Southport', about which he asked her a good deal.

At about 9 p.m. he went out for a drink, and as he walked downstairs and out into the street, she picked up an evening paper lying on the table. She could hardly believe it when the first thing to attract her attention was a photograph of a man astonishingly like the one to whom she had just been talking. There was only one discrepancy between the printed description and the reality; he had blue eyes and not brown, as the paper said. However the resemblance was so marked that she immediately went to report it at the police station.

Soon after her return Black came in, and sat down to talk again. This time, she noticed, he was eyeing her with suspicion. Her small son nearby had a piece of paper and pencil with him. He sat down and started doing a sketch of his mother, then turned to Black, saying, 'Now I will draw you.' Black smiled nervously, and as the boy looked into his face to capture his likeness, he became ever more restive. Eventually, as their eyes met, Black closed his, and he told them he was off to bed. Though he went straight upstairs he seemed unable to settle, and several times he came down again for no apparent reason. She could see he was apprehensive, and 'in dread of something'.

It was nearly midnight when two members of the Liverpool constabulary entered the hotel, and knocked on his door. A voice inside shouted, 'Who's there?' The officers demanded to be allowed in, but he refused. The officers forced the door, and found that Black had not merely locked it, but also wedged a chair under the handle. By the light of an electric torch they could see him sitting on the bed partly dressed, holding a penknife in his hand, and bleeding from a freshly inflicted wound in the throat. He sprang at them but they overpowered him and removed the knife, though only after he had succeeded in injuring himself even further and was bleeding copiously. As his condition appeared serious he was not taken straight to the police station, but an ambulance was summoned and he was taken to the Liverpool Northern Hospital, where his wounds were dressed. He had done his best to try and fulfil the prophecy (or boast) in his letter to Mr Kelly that he would not be brought back to St Austell alive.

When his hotel room was searched, it was found that he had only brought a small quantity of luggage with him, and his belongings included various articles which could have been used for effecting a disguise if needed. Only one of the photographs published by the press was said to be a good likeness, and rather oddly, it was this particular photo, which had been cut out of a newspaper and affixed to the wall of his room. Had he put it there in order to remind himself that he needed to improve on his disguise before travelling elsewhere? Though he had been described as clean-shaven, he now had a slight growth of moustache.

Once the story broke, it became apparent from police enquiries that he had visited Burnley and other towns in Lancashire. From Southport he had gone to Liverpool, where he had probably been for at least two or three days, wandering about quite freely, visiting various hotels and other establishments, looking in shop windows, behaving normally and evidently keen not to draw attention to his appearance. A porter at another Liverpool hotel, the Stork, had seen him there in the company of a woman in the smoking room, and noticed the tattoo on his wrist when he reached out to pick up a glass. The porter left the room to go and check the printed description, but when he returned Black and the woman had gone.

In hospital Black was placed under constant supervision by two members of the Liverpool police, working in turn, until he was better. He had lost much blood, and for some hours he was slipping in and out of consciousness. Within twenty-four hours he was well enough to sit up in bed and have a cigarette.

A few days later he was discharged, remanded in custody and taken to St Austell on 30 December. On arrival he presented a pitiful sight in his grey suit without collar or tie, and a black beard which he had grown in the last few weeks to hide the scar on the left of his throat. Still appearing far from well, he had a septic right leg and was too weak to walk into the guardroom at the police station without the aid of the two burly officers flanking him.

On the next day, at proceedings lasting about an hour and a quarter, he was charged at the town court with obtaining money by false pretences, two sums of £15 and £20 respectively, from another victim, George Moss, a stores manager for a manure and coal firm, for the purchase of non-existent insurance policies. Black still looked frail and ill as he was assisted into the dock by police. While part of the evidence was being read he looked as though he was on the verge of collapse, holding his throat, but he revived after a drink of water. Evidence was given that when he was asked for the policies, he assured Moss that they were at his office and that they were genuine. When charged he had nothing to say. He was committed for trial on this offence, and on a further charge of obtaining £30 from Nora Smith.

Nevertheless a much more serious matter than embezzlement had to be considered. On 21 January Black was committed for trial at Bodmin Assizes, charged with murdering his wife by the administration of arsenic. Dr Andrew said that no arsenic was present in the medicine he prescribed Mrs Black during her last illness. He denied that he had told her husband, as he had asserted, that the valves of her heart were gone, or that she was not likely to recover. After he had left home on his ostensible errand to St Austell, she seemed quite relieved that her husband had gone, and said she hoped she would never see him again. Her wish had been granted, but not in the way she might have wished.

James Webster, a senior Home Office analyst, said that he had found arsenic present in all the organs submitted to him. There was a total quantity of 3.73 milligrams of arsenic, or approximately 1/17th of a grain. His opinion was that there would not be less than ten milligrams, or about a sixth of a grain, in the whole body. In one full bottle of medicine, some ointment, and some tooth powder, he found a slight amount of arsenic, but the amount found in the medicine could not account for the quantity in the organs. The arsenic in the medicine was probably due to a slight impurity in the bismuth, and the amount found in the organs would be compatible with medicinal administration of arsenic over a considerable period.

Sir William Wilcox, physician at St Mary's Hospital and consulting medical officer at the Home Office, said that Mrs Black's symptoms had been entirely consistent with arsenic poisoning. He was sure that considerable doses of the substance were taken on 31 October, within twenty-four hours of the onset of her illness, and it was possible that poisonous drugs were given on the first few days of the illness, rather than towards the end.

After evidence was heard from Detective Sergeant McAllister of the Liverpool police, one of the officers who had arrested Black in the hotel room at Liverpool, Black asked if it was compulsory to make a statement, and was told that it was not. He was kept in custody at Exeter Gaol.

By the time the case came to trial at Bodmin Assizes early in February, public interest had reached a considerable level. That an apparently respectable member of the community could have been responsible for such crimes and sparked a manhunt well beyond the westcountry had generated a degree of curiosity not associated with any previous murder case in Cornwall for many years. Long before the judge was due to take his seat, there was a queue several hundred strong seeking admission to the Court. Only about half were allowed in, and the card 'Court full' was accordingly displayed on the Court gates. Those who could not get in at once lined up, hoping for access to resumed proceedings after the luncheon interval, but even so many of them were in for disappointment through lack of room.

The proceedings on 1 and 2 February 1922 were presided over by Mr Justice Rowlatt, the counsel for the prosecution were Mr Holman Gregory and Mr Harold Murphy, and for the defence Mr Lhind Pratt. By this time Black was in much better physical shape, according to the *Western Morning News*; 'gone was his previous dejected appearance, gone was the beard which had given him such an aged look, and gone also was much of his careworn demeanour.' Listening with evident interest to everything said by counsel and witnesses, he looked more his old self, with a black moustache, dressed in a neat grey suit with collar and tie. When charged, he replied 'Not Guilty' in a firm voice, and immediately objected to two members from the jury, a man and a woman from the St Austell district, both of whom were discharged and their places taken by two men.

The main witnesses for the prosecution were James Webster and Sir William Wilcox, who reiterated their statements made at the previous hearing. This time Webster stated that in his opinion the cause of death was arsenic poisoning; though Mrs Black had also suffered from kidney disease, 'that was not incompatible with her living for some years'.

Mr Pratt had little to offer in defence. When he asked Willcox that if Mrs Black had died from gastritis, in other words from natural causes, would the post-mortem examination have given the same negative result as it gave in this case? Wilcox agreed that it would, but said that gastritis would not have lasted as long.

Black continued to deny any wrongdoing. He told the court that he and his wife had lived happily together since their marriage, and that she had always been prone to gastric trouble. He denied that he had ever been to Timothy White's to purchase arsenic, either there or anywhere else; 'I have never had poison of any kind in my possession,' he stated categorically. Nevertheless he did admit to running away to Liverpool and attempting suicide because he was beset with financial difficulties, 'because I was placed in a rather peculiar position for the time financially', and charges were threatened against him. When asked why he had been sacked by the Refuge Insurance Company, he admitted that it was 'because I used their name illegally.'

When he was shown the poisons book, and told that the signature 'E.E. Black' was similar to his, he still denied it. Bertrand Parnell identified the signature, and the handwriting of the letter received by Mr Kelly, as being those of Black. The latter continued to deny that he ever told any of the neighbours that his wife was going to die, or that he had seen a Red Cross book in his house turned down at the section dealing with arsenic poisoning, for at least twelve months.

When his stepdaughter Marion began to gave evidence she was noticeably nervous at first. However, her confidence was restored as she proceeded to recapitulate on her former statements regarding the progress of her mother's illness. The judge asked her 'on what terms' were her parents. 'Very good', she replied, though when he asked her what quarrels there had been, she admitted there were 'several minor ones'. More damningly, she revealed that her stepfather had been forcing his attentions on her since she was fifteen years old, and continued to do so up to the time of her mother's illness. As she feared his outbursts of temper, she did not tell her mother.

Three of the female neighbours at Tregonissey who had helped to nurse Annie Black appeared in the witness box. Ann Best told the court that the dead woman had repeatedly complained of a burning sensation after taking the medicine from her husband, while Blanche Chesterfield and Mary Smith both said that Edward Black repeated a statement from Dr Andrew that the valves of his wife's heart had gone, and she was not expected to live very long.

Alfred Chubb, a clayworker and friend of Black, said that he was sitting up one night with him during his wife's illness, when the prisoner poured out a dose of medicine and took it upstairs. His wife said she could not take any more of the medicine, even if she was to die that moment. Mr Black replied that he would go downstairs and get a second dose. 'What did you understand by that?' asked the judge. 'I understood he was really forcing it on her,' was the answer. Immediately after she had taken the medicine she began to vomit. The prisoner took her another dose less than two hours later, but she objected again to having to take it, and continued to be sick nearly all night.

James Kelly referred in detail to Black's letter, which he had received from Southport in November. It said it would be 'the last letter I shall ever write in this world,' that he was heartbroken and 'could not stand it any longer', and that he was 'going to Annie, God bless her!' Later it went on to say that he could not understand why Dr Andrew did not tell the others about the state of Annie's heart as he had told it to him:

Ask him to be a man and not a cad. What does he mean by suggesting arsenic? By God, Joe, you know me better than that, and I admit I made the biggest mistake of my life when I came away. What made me do it I can't say. But we all make mistakes, old friend, and I am going to pay a big price for mine.

In summing up, Mr Justice Rowlatt affirmed that the prosecution had proved that the deceased woman died of arsenic poisoning; that the prisoner had bought some just before she died; and that while she was ill, he was the main person in attendance on her, and was the one giving her medicine. Yet there was no evidence of motive, and the only one suggested was that Mr Black might have wanted to get rid of his wife, who was considerably the senior partner in age. It was true that his behaviour all through the illness was that of a devoted man faithfully attending his wife, but that would be consistent with the argument that he wanted to keep up the appearance that his wife was dying from gastritis.

After being out for forty minutes, the jury returned a verdict of guilty. As for the other charges of fraud in connection with the insurance policies, they were allowed to remain on the files of the court. Black was sentenced to death.

The trial had attracted such interest that over a thousand people were standing outside the Court to hear the news and watch the closed cab in which the prisoner was escorted to the railway station and taken to Mutley Prison, Plymouth, en route to Exeter Gaol. Bodmin Gaol was about to be closed by the Prison Commissioners, and was not admitting any new prisoners, much to the judge's irritation. He had to ask Mr Wood, governor of Mutley Prison, why it was necessary for the prisoner to have to return to Plymouth each night during the trial. It was 'perfectly monstrous', said Mr Justice Rowlatt, and as a result of his intervention, the Home Office agreed to open a cell at Bodmin for Black on a temporary basis.

Nevertheless it was to Exeter that he returned under sentence of death. He took the case to the Court of Criminal Appeal, who considered the evidence on 6 March, but Mr Justice Avory dismissed the appeal. Edward Black was hanged at Exeter by John Ellis and Seth Mills on 24 March 1922.

Some fifty years later, crime historian Colin Wilson suggested that Black was a 'killer who owed his conviction to loss of nerve'. Whether he was guilty or not, Wilson argued, he should have been acquitted. His wife died three days after he had left home for the last time, and she might have done so at her own hand 'in despair at his desertion'. Had it not been for his folly in denying the purchase of arsenic and then declaring that 'his' signature was a forgery, he might have escaped the gallows.

16

'THEY HAD VERY SERIOUS TROUBLE'

St Teath, 1923

Annie Trenberth Osborne was a proud and private person, who kept herself to herself and had very few close friends or confidantes. The widow of Harry Osborne, she was in her mid-forties and was believed to have previously worked as a housekeeper at Trebarwith when she moved to Union Row in St Teath in 1920. With her came her twelve-year-old daughter, also called Annie Trenberth but known to everyone as Trennie.

While Annie remained aloof, Trennie, an extremely beautiful girl with flowing, waist-length hair, soon became very popular. She made many friends in the village and grew especially close to the Wallis family who were the innkeepers of the White Hart Inn, often taking on odd jobs for the family to earn a little pocket money.

In 1923, it became obvious to all in the village that Trennie was expecting a baby. Her condition was not discussed openly, and certainly not by her mother, who remained as distant as ever.

On Easter Sunday of that year, Trennie was attending church when she fell ill and was taken home by the vicar's wife. Annie declined to call a doctor and refused all offers of help and, when Trennie was next seen out and about, it was apparent that she was no longer pregnant. Yet there was no sign of a baby and Trennie looked terribly ill. Eventually, concerned villagers took matters into their own hands and two doctors were asked to visit Trennie at home. Dr Jerome from Camelford and Dr Bailey from St Tudy examined Trennie and confirmed that she had recently given birth.

The visit from the doctors seemed to throw Annie into a panic and, as soon as they had left, she was seen running round the house bolting the doors and boarding up the windows.

Shortly before the unexpected arrival of the doctors, Trennie had been visiting a friend, Annie Wallis. Annie confirmed that Trennie had previously been a little upset because people had been talking about her, but on that evening she was in good spirits and behaving in a perfectly normal manner. Annie Wallis went round to Trennie's house at about 10.15 p.m., a couple of hours after the doctors had visited. She had found all the doors locked and bolted and, when she tapped on the window, Trennie called out to her, asking what she wanted. Annie replied that it did not matter, since her friend had gone to bed. Annie and Trennie had parted with the words 'See you tomorrow', so Annie called at the house again a couple of times on the following morning. Once more, she found the doors locked and received no response to her knocks. She began to worry, wondering if Trennie might be ill and if her mother had gone to work and left her alone at home. The sight of the family dog inside the house compounded her fears, as it was unheard of for Trennie and her mother to go away and leave the dog behind. Besides, Trennie had said nothing the night before about going out . . .

On the evening prior to the doctor's visit, both Annie Trenberth and her daughter had visited Annie's brother, Aaron Ede, who had also found them normal and cheerful. He visited the house in Union Row at about 6 p.m. on the following day. Like Annie Wallis before him, he too found the doors locked and was unable to raise a reply to his knocking. He went back again a little later, but once again was unable to rouse the occupants of the house and returned home.

By midnight, his concerns for his sister and niece could no longer be ignored. When his knocking went unanswered once more, he called for the assistance of some men from the village, who brought a ladder and propped it up against the front of the house. Ede climbed up to peer in through the upstairs windows, but failing to see anything but the frantically barking dog, moved the ladder round to the back of the house. Through a small window, he could just make out a figure lying on one of the beds.

The villagers managed to break into the house through a downstairs window and Ede rushed upstairs to the bedroom. There he found both Annie Trenberth and Trennie, lying dead on a blood-soaked bed. It was obvious that the women were beyond all help, so he did not approach the bodies, but immediately left the house and sent for the police and a doctor.

The doctor who examined the bodies was the same Dr Jerome who had earlier visited Trennie and her mother. At the subsequent coroner's inquest, he refused to reveal the details of his first visit to the court, except to say that the results of his examination had been made known to both Annie and her daughter at the time and that 'They had very serious trouble'. Brushing aside questions from the jury, he insisted that he was only present to give details of the causes of death and nothing more.

He described Trennie as having had her throat cut. The wound was, he felt, too long and deep for Trennie to have cut her own throat – rather he felt that someone standing over the girl, on her right-hand side, had inflicted the injury. He was certain that the wound had been inflicted while Trennie was asleep since there were no signs of any struggle. Trennie, he believed, would have bled to death within seconds. Annie also had a wound to her throat, but this was a stab rather than a slash. The wound reached right down to Annie's spinal column and had cut through arteries, veins and the windpipe. However Annie had not died instantly. The doctor found bloody towels in front of her, suggesting that she had tried to sit up after inflicting the wound.

The coroner's jury barely needed to deliberate before returning their verdict. They concluded that Annie Trenberth had murdered her daughter Trennie, and then committed suicide.

The funeral for Annie and Trennie was attended by most of the village, with crowds of people lining the route from Union Row to the churchyard.

*The grave of
Ann Trenberth
Osborne and her
daughter at the
parish church of
St Teath.*
(© Nicola Sly)

They watched solemnly as two flower-bedecked coffins were brought from the Trenberth house and carried to the church. At the church gates, the coffins were met by the Revd Kingdon, who conducted the service. The coffin containing the body of Trennie was taken into the church, while that of her mother was rested outside and the service was conducted as though only one person was being buried. Mother and daughter were laid to rest in the same grave in the small graveyard, where a headstone, erected by Aaron Ede in their memory, now marks their passing. It makes no mention of the murder, bearing the words:

In Loving Memory
of
Anne Trenberth Osborne
of St Teath
Widow of Harry Osborne
Who died April 21st 1923
Aged 48 years

Also of
Ann Trenberth (Trennie)
Daughter of the above
Who died April 21st 1923
Aged 15 years

'At Rest Together'

It appears as though the perceived stigma of having a pregnant, unmarried daughter was simply too much for Annie Trenberth Osborne to bear and that, rather than face the shame and disgrace of an illegitimate grandchild, Annie elected to deal with the situation in her own way. After the deaths of Annie and her daughter, police searched the house and gardens at Union Row extensively, seeking the body of Trennie's baby, but no trace of the infant was ever found.

17

'BE A TRUMP, TAKE AND DO IT'

Titson, Marhamchurch, 1928

Richard Francis Roadley was an enigma. He lived in a squalid cottage in the small hamlet of Titson, near Marhamchurch, and was practically a recluse. The eighty-four-year-old bachelor was a woman-hater, and would not even allow one into his home. He was also deeply suspicious of strangers, and the only people with whom he willingly interacted were the local children. He was a retired farmer, although in name only. When farming he had not managed his land at all well and, although he purported to love horses, they had been allowed to run wild about his farm. He had sold up during the war, when landowners were forced to grow crops to support the war effort, retiring to a small cottage which soon fell into rack and ruin.

His only hobbies seemed to be reading, particularly engineering books, and attending local auctions where he regularly purchased all manner of junk on the premise that it might just come in useful one day. The interior of his cottage reflected his preoccupation with acquiring seemingly useless objects, its rooms piled floor to ceiling with clutter, so much so that the stairs were used as a series of shelves on which his possessions were precariously stacked.

To all intents and purposes, he was a dirty, rather eccentric old man, who kept himself pretty much to himself and shunned contact with the world outside his decrepit home. However, all was not as it seemed. After the death of his brother in 1927, he had become Lord of the Manor at Scotter, near Gainsborough, Lincolnshire, and was in fact very wealthy. He was known to give generously to charities and was even rumoured to support financially a children's home in the Midlands. Though he shied away from contact with the villagers near his home, he accommodated many deserving requests for financial assistance and was also in the habit of buying sweets for the local children. When one family from the village were unable to send their children on a Sunday school picnic because they did not have sufficiently respectable clothes, Roadley treated the children to cakes to make up for their disappointment. On the occasions when he ventured into nearby Holsworthy to shop, he would regularly withdraw the sum of £50 from his bank account.

On Saturday 18 February 1928, he purchased some eggs from his neighbour, paying with a shilling, which he took from a purse that, the neighbour noticed, contained more silver coins. He was not seen again until Sunday when,

Marhamchurch village.

at lunchtime, a little girl noticed that his blinds were still drawn closed. She mentioned this to Mr Hicks, Roadley's neighbour, and Hicks went to investigate.

Finding the front door of the cottage unlocked, Hicks pushed it open and heard the sound of heavy breathing. Tracing the source of the noise, he spotted Roadley's feet under a chair and when he raised the blinds to allow more light into the room, he found the old man lying on the floor, his head and shoulders tightly wrapped in a blanket. Removing the blanket revealed a large pool of blood and a wound to Roadley's forehead, oval in shape, measuring approximately 2×1½ inches. A doctor was immediately summoned and he confirmed that the injury had not been caused by a fall, but that the victim had been struck with a blunt object.

Roadley died from his injuries later that evening and the local police immediately called for the assistance of Scotland Yard in finding his attacker. Over the next few days, his cottage was subjected to a thorough search, a procedure no doubt hampered by the filthy and cluttered conditions. The police found several clues; from the soft mud outside the cottage door, they were able to obtain casts of footprints. Inside the house, the bedroom window had been obscured by bedding, presumably by the intruder to prevent lights being noticed from outside. They recovered several trunks from the cottage, the sides of which had been slit with a knife to gain access to their contents. There were also reports of a strange car, possibly a Morris, being observed in Titson shortly before the murder.

The police worked tirelessly, day and night, to secure an arrest, checking local lodging houses and workhouses and questioning anyone within a twenty-mile radius who was unable to account for their movements at the critical time. Over the next few days, two men were separately detained, one from Cardiff and the other from North Wales, and brought back to the police court at Stratton for questioning. Both were released without charge.

Then police stumbled across a clue that led them to William John Maynard, who was promptly called in for questioning. Maynard, a thirty-six-year-old rabbit trapper, lived in the nearby hamlet of Poundstock with his wife and son. He was taken to Stratton and, being unable to satisfactorily account for his whereabouts on the night of the murder, was detained at the police station while further enquiries were made. Meanwhile, officers conducted a thorough search of his home, outhouses and land, paying particular attention to the stream that ran along the bottom of a field in front of the house. Maynard's brother-in-law was forced to look on disconsolately as his recently planted potatoes and vegetables were dug up by the police and handed to him one by one.

Despite their thoroughness, the police located nothing of interest apart from an 18in adder in a hedge bottom, which was quickly killed. It was therefore decided to return Maynard to his smallholding to assist with the search. The rabbit trapper was brought home, but as he was leaving the police car heading for the fields, he dramatically collapsed and was immediately carried back to the car and driven back to Stratton. The journey was not without incident, since the police car suffered a burst tyre on the way.

Although he was examined by a doctor and pronounced fit, Maynard presented a pitiful sight. He spent his time in custody lying moaning on a rug on the floor, refusing to participate in the proceedings, even when he was charged with Roadley's murder. Seemingly incapable of answering any of the questions put to him, he was simply covered with rugs and left to his own devices. Brought before magistrates a few days later, he was still in a state of collapse, hence rather than transporting the prisoner to the courthouse, the magistrates went to the police station to conduct their hearing.

Dr Harold Holtby examined the prisoner a few minutes before the start of proceedings, and gave his opinion that the accused was able to appreciate and understand what was happening. Still, as the session began, Maynard continued to lie on a mattress on the floor, covered with a blanket, his eyes remaining tightly closed. Hauled upright to hear the reading of the charges against him, he made no response and was gently returned to his mattress. Shortly afterwards, Maynard's father and wife visited the police station. The prisoner was told that they were there and asked if he wanted to see them – again, he gave no reply.

Having been remanded in custody, Maynard was taken to Exeter Prison by car that afternoon. Before the journey, he managed to compose himself somewhat; he got up, washed and drank a cup of tea, but refused food. He also requested a blanket to cover his head while walking to the car, which he was given.

By 7 March, when he was brought before the magistrates again, Maynard had adopted a very different attitude. He was calmer, replying promptly and in the affirmative to the only question he was asked, which was whether he understood the proceedings. Before being returned to Exeter, he was allowed to see his father, brother and brother-in-law. The case was adjourned until 15 March when he again appeared at Stratton Police Court. By now, the accused was much stronger and steadier, sitting quietly in the dock occasionally stroking his chin and smiling at remarks made by his counsel.

Counsel for the prosecution, Mr Sefton-Cohen, first outlined the circumstances of Richard Roadley's murder, explaining how his body had been discovered, then went on to discuss Maynard's first statement to the police. Asked to account for his whereabouts on the night of the murder, Maynard had stated that he had eaten his tea at about 5.30 p.m. then loaded his gun, with the intention of shooting a pigeon for his Sunday dinner. By dusk, he had still not managed to bag a pigeon, so had gone to his outhouse to overhaul his gin traps in preparation for his work on Monday. From the outhouse, he went back into his home at about 9 p.m. where he found his wife in the company of a visitor, Bert Yeo. However, in a written statement, made the same evening and signed by Maynard, he seemed doubtful as to whether Yeo was actually visiting or not. Maynard's wife told a contradicting story in which she said that her husband had not been home at all on the Saturday evening. Her statement was given while Maynard was actually present in the same room and standing around 4ft away.

According to Maynard, he and his wife retired to bed around ten minutes after he had come indoors from his outhouse. Their lodger, Harold Knight, had returned home later, although Maynard had not heard him come in. On the following morning, Maynard said that he had gone to visit his father, from whom he collected a batch of papers, before returning home at between 11.30 a.m. and noon. He had spent the rest of Sunday at home where he had listened to some gramophone records.

After making his statement, Maynard was detained while the police officers tried to verify his account of his movements. However, on the following day, while still in police custody, he asked to make another statement, which was taken by Chief Inspector Prothero.

In this subsequent statement, Maynard alleged that he had arranged to meet a man named Thomas Harris in order to accompany him to Titson to try and get some money. Harris, he said, had planned the robbery some time ago and Maynard had been included in the plan. Maynard had waited outside Roadley's cottage while Harris had gone in, intending just to cover the old man with a blanket. A scuffle developed and Harris came out to tell Maynard that he had hit Richard Roadley. At this, Maynard had entered the house, finding Roadley lying on the floor of the front room. He had picked up a rug and thrown it over the old man's head before leaving the house again to keep watch.

Harris, said Maynard, had been in the house for almost three-quarters of an hour before he came out and the two walked home together across the fields. Harris had given Maynard two gold watches and a handful of silver coins, and had also returned the hammer with which Maynard had armed himself earlier that evening and which had inflicted the fatal wound on Roadley.

Early the following morning, Maynard had picked up his bloodstained boots and cap and the two gold watches. On the way to visit his father, he had thrown the boots into the stream, stuffed his cap in a rabbit hole and buried the two watches in a tin near the entrance to his father's home. He had kept the silver coins, amounting to around thirty shillings in his pockets. The hammer was later hidden in a neighbour's field.

Maynard stated that he had met Harris by chance during the following week when he had gone to Wainhouse Corner to buy groceries. Harris had told him that he had buried the money and hidden some silver. Harris' last words to him as they parted were, according to Maynard, 'For God's sake, don't split!'

Harris, a local chimney-sweep aged fifty-six, did have a criminal record, having been convicted of stealing rabbits and fowls on several occasions. As a young man, he had also been charged with unlawful wounding, but later acquitted. Fortunately for him, he had been visiting a family called Hicks at their home in the nearby village of Jacobstow and had an unshakeable alibi for the time of the murder. When interviewed by the police, he maintained that it was Maynard who had planned the robbery and, more than once, tried to persuade him to act as his accomplice. Having known Richard Roadley all his life, Harris had declined.

Maynard, it was discovered, had asked Bert Yeo to provide him with a false alibi. Yeo and his wife and children had visited Mrs Maynard at home on the night of the murder, but had left at about twenty-five minutes to nine, not having seen Maynard. Some days later, Maynard had approached Bert as he was spreading manure in his employer's field, telling him that the police were asking questions and, if asked, he should say that Maynard had been at home at about 8 p.m., then gone out to get some 'baccy'. At first, Yeo had refused to tell a lie, worried that he might get himself into 'hot water', but Maynard had persisted, saying 'Be a trump, take and do it – they will never find out'. Eventually, Yeo had reluctantly agreed and initially told the police the story that Maynard had concocted, but later retracted his statement.

John Marsh, a labourer employed by Maynard to trap rabbits, told the magistrates that, prior to the murder, he had not been paid his wages as his boss had claimed to be short of money. Immediately after the murder, Maynard had paid him in cash, drawing a handful of silver from his pocket and, a couple of days later, had handed him yet more money, which he asked him to pass on to another creditor.

Perhaps the most damning evidence of all was the fact that an apparently bloodstained cap, positively identified by Marsh as belonging to Maynard, had indeed been found stuffed in a rabbit hole, exactly where he admitted to placing it in his third statement. At this stage, the hearing was adjourned until 17 April to allow the police more time to complete their investigations.

When the hearing resumed, one of the first testimonies heard was that of Dr Roache (sometimes given as Roach or Roche) Lynch. The senior official analyst for the Home Office had been asked by police to examine three hammers, one of which had been found in the outer hall of Roadley's cottage. In addition, he had also tested a sand stone, a pocketknife, a torch and several items of clothing belonging to the defendant. He was able to state that, of the three hammers examined, one bore traces of human blood and the second and third had 'suggestions' of blood, although in insufficient amounts to allow for reliable testing as to its origin. Human blood was also found on the torch, a jacket, a waistcoat and the cap.

Even though a witness had mentioned that Maynard had cut his hand badly on a rabbit trap shortly before the murder, Lynch discounted suggestions that the bloodstains may have resulted from the defendant cutting himself, since those on the jacket in particular were too widely spread. He also denied that the stains could possibly be rabbit's blood, having specifically carried out tests to eliminate that possibility. Besides, Dr Holtby, who had examined Maynard while he was in custody, had noticed no recent cuts on his hands that might have explained the amount of blood on his jacket and other effects.

Two bank managers also gave evidence before the magistrates. The manager of the bank at Bude testified that Maynard's account was in credit at the time of the murder, but his counterpart at a bank in Holsworthy had recently written to Maynard, concerned that his account was overdrawn by £238. Maynard's critical financial situation was thought to be sufficient motive for him to commit the robbery but, shortly after the murder, he had paid £40 cash into his Holsworthy bank account, an amount that had appeased his bank manager for the time being.

The hearing was resumed the following day, this time opening with evidence given by Inspector Pill. While Pill was being cross-examined, Maynard tried several times to interrupt him, asking if he might speak. Eventually, becoming more and more agitated, Maynard broke in, asking Pill to look him in the face and say he had told the truth.

Other police officers gave evidence throughout the day, and there were particularly searching questions asked about Maynard's medical state following his collapse when taken to assist in the search. The police asserted that a doctor had been called because they were anxious to do nothing that might have been deemed unfair to the prisoner. However, when the doctor had dismissed Maynard's condition as being 'bunkum and cowardice', they had charged him with the murder. The defence suggested that Maynard, a small man, had been bullied and harangued into giving a confession.

Finally, there appeared to be some confusion about the murder weapon. The hammer found at Roadley's cottage was the only one of three tested to show positive evidence of staining with human blood. Yet, due to the shape of Roadley's wounds, it was not thought that this was the hammer that inflicted his injuries. The hammer used in the murder was believed to be one to which Maynard had subsequently directed the police, found in a field opposite his home. This bore suggestions of blood staining but in insufficient quantities for reliable testing to determine whether or not it was human or animal blood. It had, however, been used for legitimate purposes for some time after the murder, before being hidden in long grass and police were of the opinion that this may have destroyed any significant traces of blood.

Once all the evidence had been presented, the magistrates consulted together before the chairman announced that, in their opinion, there was a *prima facie* case and that Maynard should stand trial for the murder of Richard Roadley. The accused was then returned to Exeter Prison where he was held in custody pending the start of his trial, to be held at Bodmin Assizes on 1 June.

When the trial opened, Maynard pleaded not guilty to the crime. Although he seemed calm in the dock, after a break for lunch, a message was sent up to the court that the defendant was 'indisposed'. He had suffered an acute attack of hysteria and the proceedings were delayed for a few hours to allow him to recover.

In the witness box, Maynard argued that he was always a little inconsistent in paying wages to Marsh, his employee. Sometimes he was late in paying him; sometimes he paid Marsh for his work in advance. The money that Marsh had been paid after the murder, including that which he had been asked to pass on to another debtor was Maynard's own money and not the proceeds of murder. 28s had come from the sale of seven hens at 4s each and another 27s 6d had been a payment for eggs, received on the day before the murder took place.

The defendant testified that he had cut his thumb in a rabbit trap and that the wound had bled copiously, accounting for the bloodstains on his clothing and on the hammer, which he agreed belonged to him. He admitted asking Yeo to provide a false alibi, saying that he was worried as he could not account for his movements at the crucial time.

With regard to the incriminating statement made to Prothero, Maynard testified that the two Scotland Yard policemen had 'called him all the blackguards they could lay their hands on.' He admitted signing his first written statement, but maintained that the police had held his hands and forced them to make an approximation of his own signature on the subsequent statement taken by Prothero. At this point Mr Goddard, Counsel for the Prosecution, asked incredulously, 'You say they were holding your hands and made you sign?' to which Maynard replied, 'I got to, or be half killed, my lord.' Much the same evidence was presented at trial as at the hearing, but this time the defence seemed better prepared to argue their case. They contended that the third statement, in which he admitted his guilt, had not been made by Maynard but had been compiled by the police, who had then forced Maynard to sign it.

They questioned the relevance of the testimony of Maynard's two bank managers on the subject of his financial affairs. While accepting that he was heavily overdrawn at one bank, they pointed out that he owned his home, outbuildings and also a considerable number of cows and poultry. The value of his property and stock far outweighed the sum of his overdraft and, it was argued, removed money as a credible motive for robbery and murder.

The defence counsel emphasised the prior criminal record of Thomas Harris, and the court was asked why they should believe a man with a history of crime over Maynard, who had no previous convictions. Finally, they maintained that Roadley's death had not been murder at all, but had occurred because of a tragic accident. The deceased, they claimed, could easily have sustained his fatal wound by falling and striking his head.

In summing up the proceedings for the jury Mr Justice Swift maintained that, in the murder of Richard Roadley, there was no question of manslaughter, provocation or self-defence. In short, the hand that held the hammer was responsible for the death of the old man. It took the jury just forty-five minutes to decide that it was Maynard's hand. Asked if he wished to say anything, the prisoner quietly stated 'I am not guilty, my lord', leaving the judge to don the traditional square of black silk before sentencing him to death by hanging.

Maynard appealed against his conviction on the grounds that it was based on what were referred to as 'inaccuracies' in the judge's summary regarding the identification by Marsh of Maynard's cap. The appeal was heard by the Court of Criminal Appeal comprising the Lord Chief Justice (Lord Hewart), Mr Justice Salter and Mr Justice Acton.

Mr Batt, counsel for the defendant, maintained that Marsh had never sworn to the identity of the cap, and that this was a very important point of misdirection by the judge. He also queried the admissibility of the evidence from the two bank managers. When the murder took place, Maynard's finances were in a better state than they had been for a long time and he was under no pressure from the manager of the Holsworthy bank to settle his overdraft. His bungalow was worth between £600 and £700, he owned three cows, fifty or sixty hens and several hundred rabbit traps and did not consider himself hard up. He therefore had no real motive for committing the robbery. Besides, stated Batt, investigation of the crime scene had revealed a wallet still laying in plain view at Roadley's cottage, in the very room where the old man was found. The wallet contained £11 10s in notes and, if the motive for the murder had indeed been money, it was curious that the prisoner had not taken it, if he had actually been in the cottage.

Finally Batt questioned the police handling of their suspect. He argued that Chief Inspector Prothero of Scotland Yard had persuaded Maynard to be interviewed at Stratton police station. Until that moment, there was not one shred of evidence to connect him to the murder. Maynard had attended the police station voluntarily – then, after twenty-four hours in custody, without sleep, he allegedly asked to make another statement. Prothero and a second Scotland Yard officer had been alone with Maynard when that statement was taken. According to Batt, local police officers had been deliberately excluded from the room. Even though Maynard could read and write, the statement, which eventually covered nearly three pages of foolscap paper, was not in the prisoner's handwriting, and it had clearly been edited. The whole statement, Batt contended, was a result of bullying and intimidation of the suspect by the police.

The Lord Chief Justice admitted that Mr Justice Swift had made an error in his original summing up of the case with regard to the evidence concerning ownership of the cap. However, he described the mistake as being 'of the most immaterial character when regard was paid to all the circumstances of the case'. Thus, Maynard's appeal was dismissed.

He was executed by Thomas Pierrepoint at Exeter Gaol on 27 July 1928. According to the *Post* on the following day, 'There was no incident out of the ordinary and, had it not been for the fact that police officials were posted at the various entrances to the prison, one would scarcely have realised that such a gruesome drama was being enacted inside'. Yet despite this assertion, the paper went on to comment on a remarkable feature of the execution – the 'great number of crows' that perched on the prison roof at the exact time at which Maynard paid the death penalty.

18

'THEY WILL BLAME ONE OF US'

Lewannick, 1930

In 1921 two sisters, Sarah Ann Hearn, known as Annie, and Lydia Everard, known as Minnie, moved from the Midlands to the small hamlet of Lewannick, near Launceston, to look after their ageing aunt. When she died in 1926, the aunt left everything to Annie, 'in appreciation of her devoted nursing'. However 'everything' was little more than her home, Trenhorne House, so although the women had a secure roof over their heads, they had no income.

For almost four years, the two sisters lived together in the house until Minnie fell ill. Once again, Annie's nursing skills were in demand, but by this time she had made firm friends with the married couple who lived less than 200 yards away at Trenhorne Farm. Throughout Minnie's illness, William Thomas was a regular visitor, dropping off newspapers and bringing custards and junkets baked by his wife, Alice, to tempt the invalid. At one time, when the two sisters were in even more dire financial straits than usual, William even lent them £28, which was a substantial amount of money in the 1920s.

After years of suffering from gastric complaints Minnie died in 1930, leaving Annie, then in her forties, living alone. William and Alice Thomas remained friendly and supportive, often including Annie in outings and picnics. In October 1930, William's mother had been staying at the farm and needed to be driven back to her home near Bude on the north coast. Annie was invited along for the ride. She was delighted by the prospect and happily joined the Thomas's in their car, leaving Lewannick at 3 p.m. It was a very typical outing; after dropping off William's mother, the party parked their car in Bude. William went to get his hair cut, while both women walked around the shops. At 5 p.m. the three met in Littlejohn's tea rooms where William ordered tea, cakes and bread and butter. Annie had made her own contribution to the meal, producing from her bag some tinned salmon sandwiches and chocolate cake, and these were shared between them.

After tea they parted company again, with William making his way alone to the Globe Hotel. There he complained of nausea, but after a shot of whisky he felt much better. His wife was not so fortunate. When all three met up again, she complained of having a sickly-sweet taste in her mouth and asked if there was a fruit shop nearby. William found one and bought her some bananas.

The Strand, Bude, with the Globe Hotel on the right and Littlejohn's tea rooms (with white sun blinds) roughly in centre of picture, c. 1930. (Adrian and Jill Abbott)

On the drive home Alice began to feel terribly ill. William had to break the journey several times for her to be sick at the roadside, and when he kept a pre-arranged business appointment near Launceston, he returned to the car to find her in the public toilets vomiting again. As soon as they arrived home, Alice was helped to her bed and the doctor sent for. When he examined her, Dr Saunders found she was suffering pain in the stomach, coupled with a racing pulse and cramp in the legs. Hearing that she had eaten tinned salmon that afternoon, he immediately suspected food poisoning. Fortunately Alice was on hand to help and, once again, volunteered her nursing skills. She stayed at the farm for several days, cooking for William and caring for his bedridden wife.

Alice was expected to recover from her bout of food poisoning without any complications, but instead her condition gradually worsened. Some days, she would seem better, only to relapse the following day. Soon she was complaining of a tingling sensation in her hands and feet and of having no control over her limbs. When the doctor noticed she had developed cold sores on her lips and chest, he suggested that she should go into hospital, but she resisted the idea. In desperation William sent for her mother, Tryphena Parsons, who promptly arrived to help Annie with the cooking and nursing.

Despite their best efforts, Alice continued to deteriorate. At the beginning of November she rallied sufficiently to eat some mutton, potatoes, vegetables and a sweet cooked by Annie, but after eating, complained of the lingering sweet taste in her mouth. In an effort to rid herself of this sickly taste, she asked for lemon juice, which was served to her by Annie, but soon afterwards she began vomiting again and suffering from nosebleeds. On 1 November she became delirious, and her doctor was so concerned by her condition that he summoned a specialist from Plymouth City Hospital for a second opinion. Dr William Lister diagnosed arsenical poisoning and Alice was rushed into hospital, where she died three days later, aged forty-three.

William, who had been at his wife's bedside, returned home to Trenhorne Farm. There, according to Annie, he all but accused her of murdering his wife, saying, 'They will blame one of us and the blame will fall heavier on you than on me'. William was later to deny saying this, claiming to have little recollection of any conversation. He did recall asking Annie for a written IOU for the £28 she still owed him.

At a post-mortem, it was found that Alice's organs contained a residue of 0.85 grains of arsenic, consistent with her having consumed around ten grains. Since a dose of between two and four grains is normally fatal, her death certificate was issued citing the cause of death as 'Arsenical poisoning due to homicide' and also stating 'but there is not sufficient evidence to show by whom or by what means the arsenic was administered'.

Annie had an uncomfortable time at Alice's funeral. She felt that the other mourners were looking at her with suspicion, particularly Alice's brother, Percy Parsons. The latter asked about the food that his sister had eaten on her trip to Bude and, when Annie mentioned that she had provided sandwiches, informed her that the matter 'would have to be looked into'. When the funeral party returned to the farm for refreshments, Annie soon made her excuses and left.

On 10 November, William received a letter from Annie, which read:

Dear Mr Thomas,
Goodbye. I am going out if I can. I cannot forget that awful man [Parsons] and the things he said. I am innocent, innocent [sic], but she is dead and it was my lunch she ate. I cannot stay. When I am dead, they will be sure I am guilty and you, at least, will be clear. May your dear wife's presence guard and comfort you still.
Yours, A.H.

In a postscript, Annie complained that her life was nothing without Minnie. She asked that her love be given to Bessie (another sister) and begged them not to worry about her, writing; 'I am all right. My conscience is clear. I am not afraid of afterwards.' Finally, she gave instructions that her goods should be sold and her debt to Thomas paid from the proceeds.

William took the letter straight to the police who arrived at Trenhorne House, to find it locked and empty. They soon discovered that Annie had taken a taxi to Looe, and a few days later her coat and hat were found there on a cliff top. It looked as though she might have committed suicide by flinging herself over the cliff into the sea, but there was no trace of her body on the shore below, apart from a solitary shoe that was washed up on the beach.

Meanwhile, in Torquay a 'Mrs Ferguson' booked a room at a hotel, staying for one night and leaving early the following morning. She did not go far. Calling herself 'Mrs Faithful', she took lodgings in Torquay, later applying for a job as a live-in housekeeper to a local architect, Cecil Powell. Seduced by Mrs Faithful's excellent but fake references, Mr Powell hired her and, it seems, was highly satisfied with her work.

Alice Thomas's grave, St Martin's Church, Lewannick. (© Nicola Sly)

When Alice Thomas's inquest was opened on 24 November her husband was questioned about her death. William stated that, aside from the sheep dip and worming concoctions that any farmer might reasonably be expected to own, he possessed no poisons and certainly no arsenic. He also maintained that his wife had never objected to his friendship with Annie – and why should she, since he had never given her any reason to be jealous? Damningly, a member of staff at Shuker and Reed, a Launceston grocer and chemist shop, testified that he had sold an arsenic-based weedkiller to Annie Hearn in August 1928. The signature against a 1lb tin of Cooper's Powder in the shop's poisons book matched that of Mrs Hearn. Searches of poison registers in chemist's shops at nearby Stratton, Holsworthy, Liskeard and Camelford produced no sales of poison that could be directly tied to either Hearn, William Thomas or any members of the Parsons family, although Shuker and Reed's register did reveal a sale to a Mrs Uglow some eight years previously. Mrs Uglow was a sister to Mrs Thomas, and it was Mrs Thomas herself who had introduced Mrs Uglow as a purchaser at the chemist's shop. A thorough search of Trenhorne House, conducted on 20 November, had revealed no arsenic in any form.

On 26 November the inquest returned a verdict of murder by arsenical poisoning by person or persons unknown. This was enough for police to initiate a search for the missing Annie, issuing a wanted poster that described her as 5ft 3in tall, brown haired and grey eyed, with a sallow complexion. It mentioned that she walked briskly, holding her head slightly to the left, that she was well-spoken and had rather a reserved manner.

It was also sufficient cause for the police to exhume the bodies of Annie's sister Minnie and her Aunt Mary. Both bodies were found to contain arsenic, with Minnie's containing considerably more residue than that of Mary.

The possible poisonings in Cornwall were fast becoming national news and the *Daily Mail* offered a £500 reward for anyone finding the elusive Annie Hearn. Quite by chance, Mr Powell was a *Daily Mail* reader and he was also beginning to harbour suspicions about his housekeeper, 'Mrs Faithful'. He had noticed that a coat that she bought from a mail order firm had arrived addressed to a 'Mrs Dennis'. Moreover, his copies of the *Daily Mail* were being tampered with before he got to read them each morning, as someone was carefully removing all reports relating to the missing Annie Hearn.

Mr Powell alerted the police, and on 12 January 1931 Annie Hearn was detained on her way to an errand. At first she continued to protest that her name was Mrs Dennis but she eventually admitted her true identity when confronted by a police sergeant from Lewannick, Sergeant Trebilcock, who immediately recognised her. She appeared very cool and positively talkative. Superintendent William Pill took a statement from her, and almost immediately her words resulted in some confusion. Sergeant Trebilcock claimed that Annie said 'Mr Thomas used to come to our house every day with a paper. Of course, that was only a blind.' Pill and another officer present at the time did not hear her say this, and Annie later claimed that she had actually said; 'Mr Thomas used to bring a paper. He was very kind.' When describing the trip to Bude, she stated that on previous outings with William and Alice, they had always taken lunch with them. On the day she was invited to accompany them, she had cut some salmon sandwiches and chocolate cake, which she placed on the table at the café. Mrs Thomas had taken the first sandwich, Annie herself the second and Mr Thomas the third.

As for her argument with Alice's brother, Mr Parsons, at Alice's funeral, Annie said it had not really been a row. He had asked some searching questions about the sandwiches, leading her to believe that people suspected her of poisoning Alice. Thinking that either she or William was about to be charged with murder, Annie had fled, taking a taxi to Looe with the intention of killing herself on arrival. Her nerve failed her and she was unable to go through with her suicide.

Finally, Annie addressed the concerns about the roast mutton served to Alice shortly before her admission to hospital, stating that while she had cooked the meat, she had neither carved Alice's portion, nor helped with the gravy or other accompaniments to the meal.

Annie appeared on remand before Launceston magistrates no less than fourteen times. Initially charged only with the murder of Alice Thomas, on 24 February she was also charged with that of her sister, Lydia (Minnie) Everard. Minnie was described as an invalid, having previously suffered a nervous breakdown and with a long history of stomach troubles that had been variously diagnosed as chronic dyspepsia, bowel trouble, gastric ulcer, colitis and gastric catarrh. The most persistent of her symptoms was an inability to digest food. To aid digestion she was prescribed a mixture of bismuth, aromatics and pepsine, but by 19 April 1930, Minnie was complaining that the medicine was giving her pain. Her doctor Dr Gibson was surprised to hear this, but nevertheless gave her a check up, at which he noted that her heart sounded 'a little feeble'. He issued a new prescription for 'a soothing bowel mixture', but within a fortnight noted that his patient's condition had worsened and she was now vomiting.

Dr Gibson and his colleague Dr Galbraith continued to visit Minnie on a regular basis. By 4 July Dr Gibson observed that she had lost weight and was now complaining of rheumatic pains in her arms in addition to her usual digestion problems. At this time he checked Minnie for any signs of cancer, but his examinations did not reveal any malignancy. Two weeks later, Minnie was feeble and emaciated and seemed to the doctor to be only semi-conscious. She was so weak that she was unable to turn over in bed without assistance. The doctor believed that Minnie was slowly starving to death and made his concerns known to Annie. Her condition continued to worsen, until by 21 July she was barely able to speak and obviously in great pain. She died that night and Dr Gibson signed the death certificate, giving the cause of death as 'chronic gastric catarrh and colitis'. He described Annie Hearn as 'a good nurse and a devoted sister'.

Dr Roache Lynch, the Home Office analyst, testified for an entire day at Annie's hearing before the magistrates at Launceston. He explained that arsenic poisoning could be divided into three types – acute, sub-acute and chronic. Acute poisoning was normally but not always characterised by a swift death, usually within thirty-six hours of ingesting the arsenic, either through heart failure, poisoning of the heart muscle or by dehydration caused by persistent vomiting and diarrhoea. It could take two forms, either presenting with similar symptoms to gastro-enteritis or in narcotic form, which gave only transient nausea and vomiting before unconsciousness. Sub-acute poisoning could result from either one dose of arsenic or several doses given over a period of time. It began with symptoms of gastro-enteritis. The condition of the victim might appear to improve temporarily, before deteriorating into restlessness and neuritis, and culminating in unconsciousness and death. Chronic poisoning, on the other hand, gave rise to a variety of symptoms including digestive catarrh, disordered sensation and paralysis, with inflammation of the mouth, nasal passages and eyes. This would be accompanied by strange tingling sensations, almost as if the victim had ants crawling on their skin. Eventually the victim would experience a loss of power to the limbs with muscle pain and wasting. He was of the opinion that an initial dose of several grains of arsenic was administered to Mrs Thomas at around 5 p.m. on the day of the outing to Bude, and that her resulting symptoms were consistent with sub-acute arsenical poisoning.

As far as Minnie was concerned, Lynch felt that she had been administered regular small doses of arsenic over a longer period of time, possibly around seven months. He confirmed this by testing a length of her hair and showing that it contained arsenic throughout its length. Knowing the rate at which human hair grows, he was able to establish a time period over which Minnie had, in his opinion, been slowly poisoned. She was, according to Dr Lynch, a textbook case of chronic poisoning.

Once all the evidence had been heard, the magistrates retired to debate their decision. After only fourteen minutes' discussion, they returned to commit Annie Hearn to Bodmin Assizes for both offences.

The trial opened at Bodmin on 15 June 1931, with the defendant pleading not guilty to the murders of Alice Thomas and her sister, Lydia Everard. She was defended by Norman Birkett KC, assisted by Mr Dingle Foot, a future Liberal and then Labour MP. Cecil Powell paid for the expensive services of these gentlemen, generously donating the £500 reward he had received for being instrumental in Annie's capture.

The prosecution relied largely on the expert testimony of Dr Lynch. He testified that Alice Thomas had died from arsenic poisoning and that, by examining her organs post-mortem, he had been able to calculate that she had ingested a dose of ten grains. Minnie also had large quantities of arsenic in her body.

The counsel for the defence instantly refuted these findings, pointing out that the soil at Lewannick contained high levels of arsenic. Although the exhumation of Minnie's body had been carried out in a snowstorm, just a tiny amount of local soil could have contaminated the specimens taken and accounted for the high results of the tests. The doctor who conducted the autopsy at the graveside was called, and was forced to admit that he had taken no precautions against contamination, and also that Minnie's organs had been left in open jars next to her grave for over an hour.

Having planted the idea of contamination firmly into the minds of the jury, the defence team then set out to discredit Dr Lynch. Under questioning, he admitted that he had never seen or treated an actual case of arsenic poisoning, but only read about it. He conceded that the base level of arsenic in the soil at Lewannick was unusually high and that he had not taken this into account when calculating the levels of arsenic in Minnie's body. The prosecution maintained that Lynch's calculations were fundamentally flawed, since he had analysed a portion of muscle from the dead woman. He had then assumed that muscle represented about 40 per cent of the human body, multiplying the amount of arsenic accordingly. Yet when Minnie died, her muscles had been severely wasted following her prolonged illness and would have accounted for only around 15 per cent of her total body weight.

The court heard testimony from the Launceston chemist who had stated at Alice's inquest that he had sold arsenic-based weedkiller to the defendant. The defence team did not dispute this, merely pointing out that this particular brand of pesticide was bright blue in colour. It was demonstrated in court that, had it been used in the sandwiches, it would have turned the bread bright blue too.

The defence called just one witness to the stand, Annie Hearn herself. Her calm demeanour as she maintained her innocence impressed itself on the jury. She vehemently denied poisoning either Alice or Minnie, admitting only to panicking and fleeing when she feared that she might be a suspect. It had been her intention to commit suicide, but she had eventually been too afraid to go through with it and had tried to start a new life in Torquay.

Mr H. du Parcq KC was left to sum up the case for the prosecution, even though he was clearly unwell and eventually fainted in the courtroom. He pointed out to the jury that both women had died from arsenic poisoning, both after having eaten food prepared by Annie. However, on the day of her panic-stricken flight to Looe, she had allegedly worn two coats, one on top of the other. To du Parcq, this clearly negated Annie's claims that she had intended to commit suicide, proving instead that she had been bent on duping people into believing that she was dead, leaving her free to make a new life for herself. And why, asked du Parcq, should an innocent woman flee in the first place, if not to avoid justice? Annie, he maintained, was a liar. She had lied about her intention to kill herself and, by inventing new names for herself in Torquay, had also lied about her identity. It was thus probable that she was also making false claims about her innocence.

For the defence, Birkett concentrated his closing arguments on undermining the testimony of the prosecution's expert witness. Having planted doubts in the minds of the jurors by referring to the high levels of arsenic in the Lewannick soil, he proceeded to labour the point, even though his contamination theory was not strictly true. While the arsenic levels in the soil were exceptionally high, they were not present in soluble form, so they would have been unlikely to affect the test results, even if contamination had occurred. He then tried to discredit Dr Lynch, the Crown's analyst who, he pointed out 'never attended a single person suffering from arsenical poisoning, yet he spoke of the symptoms with the same confidence that he spoke of other matters.'

Finally, Birkett asked the jury to consider the supposedly poisoned sandwiches. If a packet of sandwiches was placed on a table for three people to share, how was the poisoner supposed to ensure that the intended victim, Mrs Hearn, took the right sandwich, particularly as the bread would be bright blue?

After both sides had summed up their evidence, it was left for the judge, Mr Justice Roche, to address the jury. He quickly ruled that there was insufficient evidence in the case of the murder of Lydia Everard and instructed the jury to acquit Annie Hearn of that charge. They should focus instead on the murder of Alice Thomas, asking first if her death was due to arsenical poisoning and, if they decided that it was, did the defendant administer that poison?

Annie's guilt or innocence was dependent on whether the jury believed that she had administered arsenic to Mrs Thomas in the sandwiches eaten on the outing to Bude. If indeed the sandwiches had been laced with arsenic, then only two people could possibly have been responsible – Annie Hearn or William Thomas. The judge pointed out that it was up to the prosecution to satisfy the jury that the poisoner was not William Thomas, rather than the responsibility of the defence to satisfy them that it was. The jury deliberated for less than an hour before acquitting Annie Hearn of Alice Thomas' murder and were then instructed by the judge to acquit her of Minnie's murder as well. Within minutes Annie was a free woman again, vowing to settle her affairs in Cornwall, then never to set foot in the county again. However her innocence was not as clear-cut in the minds of the jury as their verdict suggested. One juror was allegedly heard to say later in a public house that the jury had believed that Annie and William Thomas had acted together in murdering Alice. They had found Annie not guilty, even though they felt that she had committed the murders, because they had not wanted to see her 'swing' on her own.

As there was insufficient evidence to link William Thomas to the deaths, he was never charged with the murder of his wife. Nobody but Annie was ever charged, and the murder remains unsolved.

The case has become something of an enigma in the annals of true crime. Was there ever more than friendship between Annie and William and, if so, was Alice Thomas the only obstacle that stood in the couple's way? If their relationship was, as both claimed, merely friendship, then what motive did either William or Annie have for murdering either Alice or Minnie? And, was Minnie murdered at all, or was her early death simply the consequence of a long-standing battle with illness? Was William in any way to blame for his wife's death? Or did Annie Hearn literally get away with murder?

19

'I DID NOT DO IT WILFULLY'

Bude, 1931

Mr and Mrs Herbert Crisp were the proprietors of Pentowan Hotel, Summerleaze Crescent, Bude, one of the few establishments in the holiday resort area which in the early 1930s remained open all the year round. It was a modest family-run business, and they only needed to employ the minimum of staff.

An elderly member of the family, Mary Ann Dunhill, whom they called 'Granny', lived with them. The widow of a Sheffield chemist, aged seventy-nine at the time of her death, she had been living with them since 1916. She was the aunt-in-law of Mrs Crisp, and as she had a small private income of her own, she neither needed to nor was obliged to undertake any duties at the hotel. Nevertheless, as she was in excellent health for her age, she enjoyed lending a hand with housework and such light duties as dusting and making beds. She was a regular worshipper each Sunday at St Michael and All Angels Church in the town and was often seen shopping nearby.

Early on 7 February 1931 the Crisps left the hotel for Bude station, to catch a train for Exeter where they were going to visit their son. They returned at around 9. 15 p.m. that evening, getting back to the Pentowan after fifteen minutes' walk.

Summerleaze Crescent, Bude, in the 1920s. (Adrian and Jill Abbott)

Summerleaze Crescent, Bude, 2006. (© Nicola Sly)

As a rule they left an electric light burning in the hall of the double-fronted house, and when they approached, they were surprised to see the building in darkness. The front door was locked, and increasingly anxious, they went to the back of the building to gain entry. As they walked through the ground floor, the place seemed strangely silent. They called out to 'Granny', but there was no answer.

Mr Crisp ran upstairs to her room, to find wardrobes ransacked, drawers open and their contents strewn across the floor. Even so, he was unprepared for what caught his eye next. Lying on the floor, bound hand and foot, was the body of Mrs Dunhill. He felt for a pulse, but she was cold and must have been dead for several hours.

Hurrying to the telephone, he called the police and Dr John Alfred Pontin. The latter arrived first, loosened the bindings and gags on the dead woman, and confirmed that her death had taken place between around eight and twelve hours earlier. A gag had been forced tightly down her throat, while a white apron had been thrust around her face and pushed into her mouth as a further gag. It had been tied so fiercely that her nose was bent round until it touched her cheek, and pressure on the nose and mouth had resulted in a bruise on the lower side of her jaw. Over the apron enveloping her head and neck was a counterpane which had been taken from the bed, and over the top of this was draped a tightly bound thick eiderdown, also from the bed. It was established that she had died from suffocation. Her hands were crossed at the wrists, and like the legs they were bound with an assortment of clothing snatched from the chest of drawers in the bedroom, including scarves, ties, handkerchiefs, and a pair of suspenders similar to those worn by men to keep up their golf stockings, with brightly coloured tassels attached. Mr Crisp identified them as his property. Meanwhile her luncheon, prepared by one of the servants – a dish of three baked jacket potatoes and a helping of bread and butter pudding – remained untouched on the dining room table.

When the police arrived, her bedroom was immediately locked. A motive had to be established for her murder; if done in furtherance of robbery it had been pointless, as there was very little in the way of money or valuables in the room. What there was remained untouched in the drawer where it had been placed by Mrs Dunhill. None of the other hotel bedrooms had been disturbed. In the bedroom where her body was found, Mrs Crisp's jewellery and other valuables were still in a small canvas box on the dressing table, but had not been touched either. The few other articles of value on the premises, including silver cigarette boxes and ornaments on an occasional table in the drawing room beside the fireplace, were also still in place.

When the Crisps had left the hotel that morning, their chef and handyman Joseph Samuel Cowley was in charge of the premises. Aged twenty-nine, he had worked there as kitchen porter and assistant chef since June 1929. His family background and previous history were impeccable. He had previously lived with his parents at Bridge Street in Hereford, and sung there with the choir at St John's Parish Church, where his father Arthur was sexton for forty years. One of his uncles had been Conservative agent for Hereford and later for Stratford-on-Avon, and another was head chorister at Hereford Cathedral. After leaving school he had worked for a baker in Hereford, and following a period of unemployment he took several different short-term jobs throughout the country, including a spell as a miner in South Wales, after which he moved to Bude.

Though he had never worked in a hotel before he was punctilious, reliable and good-humoured. Among his duties were preparing meals for the family, and taking sole charge of the hotel when the Crisps needed to be away for a short time out of season, as they had on this occasion. He was paid £1 a week and all meals were provided. Mrs Crisp had taught him how to cook a plain dinner, and one job in which he took considerable pride and pleasure was to take Mrs Dunhill her breakfast in bed each morning on a tray.

As the number one suspect a search was mounted for Cowley, and initial police inquiries revealed that he had asked about trains from Bude earlier in the day. When told that there were none until 4 p.m. he began to walk towards Holsworthy. Mr J. Parkhouse of Bude, who had driven to Holsworthy and back that day with his nephew Frederick, told police that they had passed a smartly-dressed man in a blue serge suit strolling along the road, and Frederick recognised him as Cowley. They were surprised to see him on foot such a distance away, but he seemed to be enjoying his walk, so they did not offer him a lift. On their return journey they passed him again, and as far as they could recall he was not carrying a suitcase or anything similar. Further inquiries suggested that on reaching Holsworthy, he had begun to walk in the direction of Launceston when he was overtaken by a bus for Plymouth, which he then boarded.

Cowley was well known in Bude, especially among the tradespeople, making regular shopping expeditions for the Crisps. He had previously had a girlfriend who was also an employee at the Pentowan, but she had since left and married. In September 1930 he had become close to Lily Neilson, who lived at Waterloo Street, Plymouth, but had come seeking work in Bude and was now employed as cook and housekeeper at the nearby Erdiston Hotel. As the person who knew him probably better than anybody else, Lily Neilson would inevitably be needed for questioning. When the police contacted her, she told them that on the morning of 7 February he had visited three business premises in the town before calling at the Erdiston to chat to her, and to invite her to tea with him.

Early the next morning she was able to provide a vital clue as to his whereabouts. At about 10.30 a.m. on Sunday 8 February he rang her at the Erdiston, saying he was calling from Plymouth. She immediately informed the police, who contacted their colleagues at the Plymouth Constabulary. Detective Inspector Lucas decided to drive through Pennycomequick to Milehouse and St Budeaux, accompanied by Detective Sergeant Hutchings. As they drove towards Milehouse they saw a man walking from the St Budeaux direction, answering the description they had been sent. The police car drove past and then very cautiously turned round so the officers could overtake him, then they got out of the car, and approached him. He made no attempt to run away, and admitted his name. When they said they were going to take him to Plymouth police station, he said he was innocent. They cautioned him, then told him that an elderly lady had been murdered at Bude where he was employed.

'I am innocent,' he repeated. 'I was too fond of the old lady to do her any harm.' He was assisted into the police car and driven to the central police station in Plymouth. Later that day Superintendent Pill from Launceston and Inspector E.W. Norrish of Stratton travelled to Plymouth and took Cowley back to Stratton, where he was formally charged with the death of Mrs Dunhill.

Already word had started to spread around the area, and there was some excitement when it became known that Cowley was going to be brought to the police station. In spite of heavy rain, a considerable crowd gathered around. Most people who had known him regarded him as a hard-working young man, the last person they would have suspected of murder. Eager for any kind of excitement, some at least must have regarded the wait as worth their while as they had a good view of him when the police car arrived. Still smartly dressed, when he stepped out of the vehicle he looked round before walking up the pathway through the garden adjoining the station, and Superintendent Pill ushered him in through the front door.

At 12 noon on 9 February he appeared before two Justices of the Peace, Mr J. Treleven and Mr C.H. Rattenbury, in the Stratton police station. Also present were Superintendent Pill, Inspector Norrish, Mr G.L. Andrews, Clerk to the Magistrates, and three representatives of the press. When he appeared from the cell he was without his jacket, his shirt sleeves were rolled up to the elbows, and as he was wearing no braces he was constantly hitching his trousers up to his waist.

Mr Andrews read out the charge of murder, and then Superintendent Pill addressed the court. He told them that as a result of a telephone message on Saturday he had gone to Bude, and in a bedroom at the Pentowan Hotel had seen the body of Mary Ann Dunhill. After further inquiries, Cowley had been detained in Plymouth the following day, and he asked for the prisoner to be remanded in custody for eight days. The magistrates said they would grant the remand and asked Cowley if he understood what was happening. He answered in the affirmative and was granted legal aid under the Poor Persons' Defence Act. The proceedings were over in a few minutes.

On 17 February he attended another brief hearing before the magistrates at Stratton, when he was remanded in custody a second time. A third appearance before the Stratton police court came on 23 February, and his statement to the police following his arrest was read to those on the bench. In this he said that he was at the hotel with Mrs Dunhill on 7 February, the day that Mr and Mrs Crisp went away. He did his usual duties around the house until about 11 a.m., then went to the lounge to talk to Mrs Dunhill and tell her he was going out on an errand. On the way back he called into the Erdiston and chatted briefly to his girlfriend. Returning to the Pentowan, he took the dogs out for a few minutes.

Returning to the hotel, he was preparing for dinner when Mrs Dunhill called to ask him to fetch a bucket of water and a chamois. He did so, then went back to the kitchen while she came out and started sweeping the stairs. While in the kitchen 'a thought suddenly came over me to do a bunk, as I thought it would be a good opportunity to do so while Mr and Mrs Crisp were away'. He went into his room upstairs and got his things together, but when he checked in one of his drawers he found he only had about 2½d. Then he thought he would 'do a robbery', took a tool from the Crisp boy's workshop, went into the office and forced open the desk where he expected to find money, but could only lay his hands on 6d in coppers in an envelope. Going into Mrs Dunhill's room he rummaged through her drawers, and in one he found her handbag which contained a £1 note and 4s. He took it all, then ransacked the rooms in a vain hunt for any more cash. Going into Mr Crisp's bedroom, he proceeded to go through the chest of drawers there.

'Mrs Dunhill heard the commotion and came in,' he continued. 'She asked me what I was doing and also said I had been in her room, then she said she was going to fetch somebody as I must have lost my head. I caught her by the throat and she fell back to the floor so I tied her up and then went to my room, put my hat and coat on and started to walk away, but after going about ten yards I turned back and went into the house. I went upstairs to look at Mrs Dunhill again. I could hear that she was still breathing. I felt her arm, she was still warm. It was then a quarter past one when I got back into the kitchen, so I thought she would be all right then and thought I had time to catch a train before someone discovered her and what I had done. I went down to the station, found the booking office wasn't open so I went into the refreshment room and had a small glass of ale and then started to walk to Holsworthy.'

Reaching the town at 4.20 p.m., he made inquiries and found there would be no train or bus to Plymouth, so he started to walk to Launceston. About four miles before the town a bus overtook him, so he stopped it and it took him to Plymouth. He spent the night there, hoping all the time that someone would have been to the hotel and found out what had happened. He was out again at 8.15 a.m. on Sunday, tried to find his way to London, but after walking some distance lost his way, and turned back. On the way he saw a place with a telephone office where there was a service for Sundays and nights only.

He went in and rang the Erdiston, asking for Lily Neilson. When she came to the phone, he asked if she had heard any news from the Pentowan. 'You should know,' she replied.

'What is it?'

She explained that Mrs Dunhill's body had been found and it clearly looked like a case of murder.

'Do they think I did it?'

'The thing speaks for itself. You have run away. Why did you?'

'I got scared.'

'It is not fair you leaving me here with all these policemen after me. The best thing you can do is to come right back.'

He promised he would return to Bude. When she asked him where he was he told her he was in Plymouth, but when she tried to find out where he was staying, he said 'nowhere'.

On leaving the office he asked the way to the nearest police station, only to be told there was not one nearby, but he might find a policeman at a telephone box by some schools. He was making his way there when a car pulled up alongside him.

When questioned as to Cowley's character, Mr Crisp said 'he was a very good servant and absolutely trustworthy.' As for the prisoner's attitude towards Mrs Dunhill, the proprietor affirmed that he 'was considerate and kind to her'. Dr Pontin gave evidence with regard to being called to the hotel and seeing her body in the bedroom. He described the scene with her head enveloped in an eiderdown, a counterpane and a window curtain, these articles being tied 'firmly' around the head with handkerchiefs knotted together and plus-four garters.

'Very firmly?' asked Ross Pashley for the prosecution. 'Yes,' the doctor replied.

At this point Anthony Hawke, leading the case for the defence, broke in. 'With due respect to my friend, I must say that this is the most leading question I have ever heard and I hope the Bench will have taken due notice of it.' Mr Pashley duly expressed his regret for having done so.

After listening to the evidence Mr A. Dickinson, who was presiding at the hearing, announced that Cowley would be tried at the Bodmin Assizes.

While in prison, he wrote to Lily, asking her,

> if you will, when the time comes, to say a few words in my favour. You know, kid, I have got myself in a terrible mess this time but believe me, kid, I did not do it wilfully. When I phoned you from Plymouth and you told me Mrs Dunhill had been murdered I was taken aback as I thought someone would have found her and brought her back. When you see Mr and Mrs Crisp try to make them believe that what happened was done on the spur of the moment and that no thought to kill was in my mind. Now, dear, I think I have said about all; one word of hope from you will mean a lot to me.

He appeared before Mr Justice Roche at the Bodmin Assizes on 24 June, with Mr J. Trapnell and Mr Dingle Foot, counsel for the prosecution, and Mr Hawke and Mr H. Elam for the defence, pleading not guilty to murder. When questioned by the prosecution, he agreed that he had committed a robbery, but said he was 'too fond of the old lady to do her any harm'. He admitted that when she caught him red-handed in Mr Crisp's bedroom and threatened to give the alarm he attacked her, took her by the throat, threw her down and tied her up, and that on his own statement there was no dispute that he did what was alleged against him. It never occurred to him that she would die as a result.

'It does not look as if you did it on the spur of the moment when you tied those handkerchiefs together?' asked Mr Trapnell.

'It was done in a hurried fright.'

'You knew there was not the slightest chance of her being alive if she were not discovered before night?'

'I was hoping she would be discovered before.'

'Why did you want to "do a bunk"?' asked the judge. Cowley admitted he did not know.

Superintendent Pill revealed that Cowley's previous record was not unblemished. While living at Hereford he had been convicted at the Petty Sessions on a charge of drunkenness, and at Axminster Police Court in 1929 he had been sentenced to one month's hard labour after being charged with loitering with intent to commit a felony.

Mr Hawke asked for a verdict of manslaughter to be returned. In his summing up, Mr Justice Roche said it was plain that the woman's death was the result of the prisoner's actions, and he was quite properly charged with murder, as there was nothing else with which he could be indicted. However, it did not follow that the jury had heard all the facts of the case that they were bound to convict the accused of murder. They had the choice of finding him guilty of manslaughter. The judge added that it was unfortunate Cowley never had the chance of being in the army, 'where they would make him do something, and exercise discipline upon him. The crime is very prevalent among youth who were disciplined during the war.'

The jury retired for fifteen minutes, and came back with a unanimous verdict of manslaughter. Cowley was sentenced to seven years' penal servitude. Most other killers of the time would almost certainly have been executed in similar circumstances, unless the defence could have argued successfully that they were insane at the time or had a history of mental illness. At no stage during the proceedings was any such suggestion made.

Although he had probably not planned to murder Mrs Dunhill, he had deliberately attempted to rob his employers, a crime in which he had been thwarted by their forethought in leaving only the minimum of cash around. He had then brutally attacked an elderly lady when she caught him in the act, and was surely intelligent enough to realise that when he assaulted her, tied her up and gagged her, then went away leaving her alone in the house, the likelihood was that she would die, either from her injuries or from shock. As a jury would be asked at the end of another murder case in Cornwall some twenty years later, was the young man they saw in the dock mad or bad?

Joseph Cowley was certainly not mad. He could thus count himself as one of the more fortunate prisoners to be put on trial for murder and step down from the dock without a sight of the judge's dreaded black cap.

20

'THEY ARE GONE AWAY FOR GOOD'

Tuckingmill, 1937

In March 1931 Philip Edward Percy Davis married Wilhelmina Vermadell Blee at Exeter. She was aged twenty-seven and he was three years younger. They lived in Exeter for a short time before moving to a house in Market Street, Hayle, where she had been born and brought up, her late father having been a carpenter in the town. Philip came from the north country; he had served with the army in India, and unable to find work at home after leaving the services, he was one of a number of men sent from Lancashire to Cornwall under a government scheme for unemployment relief.

Despite a troubled adolescence, a difficult home background with his stepmother and a short spell in a mental institution (of which more will follow), he was to all outward appearances a relatively normal young man. After leaving the army he became a skilled labourer by trade. Reserved and quiet, but pleasant, he was a hard worker, methodical and generally of smart appearance, but inclined to be impatient with his wife who was in many ways his opposite. Differences between them had become all too apparent not long after their wedding, and worsened after she gave birth to two sickly daughters. She suffered from post-natal depression and became lethargic, overweight and uninterested in her appearance. Her health had never been strong, and she took to spending more time lying in bed instead of preparing meals and doing the housework. As he worked hard in order to support the four of them, at a time when work was often hard to come by, he had little time for what looked like laziness on her part. At length he had had enough, and after four unhappy years he walked out on her.

Wilhelmina called in the police to find him. He was traced to Coventry, and brought back to Cornwall under a warrant for maintenance. Though he agreed to give their marriage another try, tragedy intervened. Their first daughter died in 1934, and her younger sister followed her to the grave in the closing weeks of 1936. He had been very fond of them, and while both parents were reeling from the loss of their second child, they were also hit by the sudden death of Wilhelmina's brother-in-law. As a widow with a fifteen-year-old daughter Monica to look after, her sister Norah had to work and she was offered a live-in post as head housemaid at Belmont Nursing Home, Southernhay, Exeter. Under this arrangement it would not be possible for Monica to share her mother's

Wilhelmina Davis and her niece Monica Rowe. (Western Morning News)

accommodation, so it was arranged that the girl would live with her uncle and aunt at Hayle, and Norah would pay them £2 a month for her keep.

This new arrangement brought some light relief into the gloomy Davis household. Unlike her aunt, Monica was very thin, tall for her age, and still rather immature, spending most of her time playing with dolls. It would not have been surprising if her uncle and aunt had resented her presence, having just lost their own children, but they became very fond of her. She had a certain childish charm, and managed to coax a regular smile out of the dour Philip Davis, which was probably more than his wife had managed for a long time.

Around Christmas 1936, Wilhelmina was admitted to hospital. A break for husband and wife from each other was probably just what they needed. Around the same time, Philip's fortunes improved when he found a job as a turner and fitter at the Climax Rock Drill & Engineering Works, Carn Brea, working on the night shift from 10 p.m. and returning home at 8 a.m. next day to catch a few hours' sleep. He and Monica left their rented accommodation at Hayle and moved into a better house in Pendarves Street, Tuckingmill, only a few minutes' walk from his works and close to the general store, run by William Andrew, his new landlord. Philip enjoyed the work and was soon recognised by his superiors as a good employee, even though his fellow workers might find him unusually quiet and inclined to keep too much to himself, preferring to go for a cigarette and a good read during breaks rather than socialise and take part in the general works camaraderie.

When Wilhelmina returned to her husband and settled into the new home that spring, she found it hard to adjust. Coming out of a lengthy spell in hospital into a different house came as rather a shock. It was doubtful whether her husband could have afforded a housekeeper, but Monica apparently kept everything in order satisfactorily in her absence. Though she had been rather immature when

Pendarves Street, Tuckingmill. (© Nicola Sly)

she moved in with them, perhaps the absence of her aunt provided an incentive to grow up quickly and take on the necessary domestic responsibilities her uncle expected.

How all three of them adapted to life together at Tuckingmill, or did not adapt, would remain a mystery. All that is known for certain was an event which would soon make local and even national headlines.

At about midday on 22 April Mr Andrew called round at the Davis' house to do some repairs to the chimney. He knocked at the door and Davis appeared, looking very haggard. He asked what chance there would be of renting the adjacent garage, separated from the house by a wire fence. Andrew said he would have to give it some thought, as he liked to store his things in there. Davis, he went on, had never expressed any interest in the garage when they were discussing rental of the house. That garage, he said, was worth a good deal to him, and he doubted whether Davis would be prepared to offer the kind of rental he was expecting.

Davis told the landlord that he had made enquiries and been given a figure of around £9 a year. Andrew said he never remembered them discussing that, but Davis still wanted to use it as workshop, and keep his lathe there. Andrew promised to give the matter some thought.

During the night shift on 23 April, Davis asked for a private word with James Simpson, his next door neighbour, who worked alongside him. Having always found him so taciturn before, Simpson was quite taken aback. Davis looked particularly shattered, had been smoking incessantly and for the first time since starting the job, had fallen asleep over his lathe.

Davis then explained that his wife had left him and gone away with Monica, taking a lot of his money with her. He had gone to bed at 2 p.m. the previous day, and when he got up to go to work, he found a note on the table saying they had left. Simpson commiserated with him, assuring him that they were bound to return when the money ran out, but Davis was adamant that his wife had told him he would never see them again. Simpson asked if she had any relatives, and Davis mentioned Monica's mother in Exeter, but was sure they would be somewhere else. The note, he went on, said 'don't bother to contact Norah, because we have no intention of going there.' He was going to write to his sister-in-law to ask if she would come and keep house for him. Meanwhile, would Simpson ask his wife if she would look after him for a day or two?

Simpson refused to commit himself. After the night shift was over, Davis arrived at his neighbour's back door and asked his wife Eliza whether her husband had told her the bad news. Mrs Simpson invited him in for a cup of tea and invited him to join them for breakfast. When he told her the sorry story, she immediately offered to help until Norah arrived.

Davis refused her offer, saying he could not possibly put her to such trouble. Instead (undoubtedly aware that what he was about to suggest would be far more trouble), he said he would rather not go home, but preferred to stay with the Simpsons instead. Mr Simpson broke in, saying that was out of the question, as his father-in-law Fred Warrener was sleeping in the spare room. Davis then very generously conceded that he would not mind sleeping on the couch instead. The Simpsons realised that here was a man who would not take no for an answer, and at length they reluctantly said he could sleep in her father's bed that day, inferring that he ought to go home after that.

That evening the two colleagues went to a union meeting together and returned to the Simpsons' house for an evening meal. Afterwards Mr Simpson got ready for the night shift, but Davis said he would not go to work, as he was feeling unwell. Mr Simpson told him firmly that much as they sympathised with his domestic problems, they had explained that they could not put him up, and they wanted him to go back to his own home – right now. When Davis said he would 'rather stay here,' the Simpsons saw they had met their match, and Warrener magnanimously said he would share his bed with Davis that night. Once again, it was implied that this was a special favour for one night only, but matters did not work out as they had imagined.

Having got himself into the house, Davis proceeded to stay for six days. Although he went back to work as normal, for the rest of the time he hung around the house making a nuisance of himself, and generally getting on Mrs Simpson's nerves. He smoked, read, sat around brooding and looking generally very depressed. Anxious to help within limits, Mrs Simpson thought he might feel better if given a chance to talk about his difficulties, and tried to encourage him to get things off his chest. But she was rather startled when he told her that although his wife had run off with £15 of his savings he was not sorry she had gone, as he had 'had a lot to put up with' before that. She was lazy and could not be bothered with housework or cooking much of the time. At this she felt so uncomfortable that she probably regretted having ever broached the subject in the first place.

Nevertheless, while imposing himself on his unfortunate neighbours, he made a few visits to his own house next door. He called in at Mr Andrew's shop to ask again about renting the garage, and was told he could do so for 4s 2d a week. The landlord handed him one of the keys, saying his son had the other, so they would keep it and let him have it after they had moved their stuff out. They cleared several items out during the next two or three days, then on 27 April he turned up again to ask the son for the second key. Once again, he got his own way.

On the next day Mrs Andrew asked for the second key back, saying they needed to remove the rest of their things. Davis stalled, saying he would let her have it the following day.

Meanwhile, on 27 April Mrs Simpson had noticed him cutting the wire fence between the back door and the garage. She questioned him about this, and he said that he had done it to make a short cut for Mr Andrew. Next morning he mentioned to Mr Andrew that he would be away for the day, and told Mrs Simpson he planned to do some gardening, and tidy things up before his sister-in-law came to stay. He spent some time moving earth and stones from the garden, using a fire shovel and a bucket. Fred Warrener saw him working and called out to ask if he would like to borrow a spade, but Davis declined, saying he would be getting some proper tools at the weekend. Warrener thought this rather peculiar, and told his daughter. Later Davis returned to the Simpsons' house for a rest. They thought he did not look at all well, and he refused an offer of food, preferring to go straight to bed.

At 9.30 that evening he said he was going to the pub. Within ten minutes he was back, saying that the beer had upset his stomach, and he thought he would be unable to go to work that night. Nevertheless he turned up for the night shift as normal.

When he returned from work on the morning of 29 April, he called at the shop to hand back the spare key, saying he had removed everything from the inspection pit for their convenience. Mr Andrew thanked him, adding casually he had heard that his wife and niece had left him. Davis asked him sharply who told him. Someone must have mentioned it in passing, said Mr Andrew. They had not come round to the shop at the weekend to pay the bill, and they had put no order in for groceries to be sent to the house that week. Davis then admitted they had left. 'They are gone away for good.'

Like Mr Simpson, Mr Andrew told him reassuringly that they were bound to return when the money had run out. Davis shook his head, saying they had taken a lot of money with them and would never return, and that he hoped his sister-in-law would be coming down to keep house for him. Once she did, he would settle the outstanding account. Then he went back to the Simpsons' house and wrote to Norah:

I have some startling news for you, and it is that Willie has left me and taken Monica with her, and she says I shall not find her through you, as she does not intend to correspond with you. She went last Wednesday night before I came down to go to work on the 22nd.

I am at present staying next door, and I want to know, Norah, if you will be a dear and come and look after me, as it will be much better than working all the morning and night up there. You can have everything you want, as I have a good job, and I am earning £4 a week. If you would do this for me you could come down on Saturday, the 28th [sic]. I will met you at the train.

Hoping this is not too great a shock for you, dearest, ever your loving brother.
P.S. Write by return and do not forget the address.

When Mr Andrew returned to collect the rest of his property from the garage he was surprised to find it so neat and tidy, with no trace of the earth or stones that Mr Simpson had mentioned. To satisfy his curiosity he began removing some of the railway sleepers that covered the inspection pit, and found some earth and rubble underneath. This struck him as odd, particularly in the light of Davis's behaviour and recent circumstances, and he went to fetch Mr Simpson. Between them they moved some more of the sleepers from the pit, which was about 5ft deep. Mr Simpson then went down the stone steps into the pit and scraped away some more soil until he could see some sacking and rags.

To his horror, next he found a human hand protruding from the earth, and the air was suddenly filled with a repulsive smell. He walked back up the steps out of the pit, and both men replaced some of the sleepers, locked the garage, and went to notify the police. Superintendent Hosking, Sergeant Rogers and Sergeant Stone arrived to come and see for themselves. Rogers went into the garage and removed some more earth from the pit, to find a blanket and a sheet, then part of a human body. It was obvious that they had discovered Wilhelmina and Monica.

The two sergeants then went to the Simpsons' house, and found Davis apparently asleep in the bedroom. Rogers shook him, and he sat up, asking them what they wanted. Sergeant Rogers cautioned him.

'I know what you want,' Davis answered sleepily. 'You know me and you know my wife. Well, I done the both of them in with a hammer. What made me do it I don't know. I have been to a mental home and we had a row the night before I went to work.'

When told that he would be detained at Camborne police station on suspicion of having caused their deaths, he asked what he ought to wear, as the clothes at the end of his bed were only his working clothes. Rogers told him they would be all right, and he got dressed. 'They didn't suffer,' he went on. 'I hit them on the head with a hammer, and they are both out there in the pit.'

When charged at Camborne police station by Sergeant Stone that afternoon, Davis said, 'You know my wife. What a big person she was. Well, we could not get on and I wish I never saw her. I suppose Andrew told you all about it, because I live in his house and take the garage from him. That's why I had the garage to put them in. I dragged them there. She used to stay in bed until 11 o'clock some mornings. I came home from work one morning and found her in bed and I did it then. What chance do you think I have got?'

The sergeant told him that if he wanted advice on the matter, he should apply to his legal adviser.

'I have been to a mental home,' Davis continued, 'and I suppose I must have been out of my mind. You can get the hammer from over the works. It is in my tool box. The key is in my trousers pocket in my bedroom.'

Meanwhile the police had gone back to his house. Superintendent Hosking, the county pathologist Dr Denis Hocking, the Camborne police surgeon Dr Blackwood, Sergeant Rogers and a photographer were investigating the scene of the crime. A bloodstained shirt and jacket had been found inside the house, and a towel (which had probably been bloodstained as well at first) had been washed and hung out to dry. The bodies of the dead women were found side by side, lying underneath a blanket with stones packed all around them, and the area beneath them was stuffed with bedding and clothes.

Wilhelmina Davis's body was covered with a white sheet, coat and pillow, all heavily stained with blood, and clothed in a vest and nightdress, her head wrapped in clothing, with one stocking knotted around the head and another round the neck, both pulled tightly; her wrists were bound with a strip of blanket and there was a length of rope around the legs. As Davis had said, his wife was 'a big person', and although only 5ft 6in tall she weighed 15st and 9lbs. It would have required some effort for a man of his slender physique to haul her down the stairs and into the garage pit. Maybe he was stronger than he looked, but he had probably made his task easier by dragging her on to an eiderdown, also found in the pit, by the rope around her legs.

The slightly-built Monica was the same height as her aunt but weighed a mere 6st 13lbs, less than half as much. She was in a curled-up position in the pit, lying on her left side, clothed in a vest, brassiere, dress and dressing gown, and also covered in a coat. Her head was wrapped with the skirt of the dressing gown, secured around the neck with a tightly knotted stocking. When this was taken away she was found to have a gag in her mouth, and her jaw was firmly closed with a leather belt fastened under her chin and over the top of her head. She too had head injuries, which had probably caused unconsciousness rather than death, and she had been suffocated, but the pathologist thought that she would have died less quickly. As she would have been much easier to carry, her uncle had probably flung her over his shoulder once she was dead.

The inquest was opened by Barry Bennetts, the County Coroner, in the Council Buildings, Camborne, on 30 April. Norah Rowe was present to confirm the identity of the victims. Dr Hocking estimated that they had been dead for between five and seven days, the actual cause of death being asphyxiation following severe blows to the head. They both had bruising to the scalp, and the bridge of Wilhelmina's nose was broken. Damage to the brain and internal bleeding inside the skull in both cases was minor, and would have caused unconsciousness but not death.

News of the discovery soon spread, and a constable had to be stationed on duty outside the garage to keep back the crowds which had gathered around out of curiosity. When the funeral of the victims took place at All Saints' Church, Roskear, on 1 May, extra police were placed on duty again. Neighbours were shocked, and several spoke to the press of the accused as 'a man of superior appearance and address, with quiet manners', his 'soldierly bearing' and 'gentlemanly behaviour'. Meanwhile the subject of their conversation was remanded in custody at Exeter Prison.

What was his motive for the double murder? When both women were killed Wilhelmina was in her nightclothes, and Monica was partly dressed. If Davis and his rather attractive niece had been carrying on with each other while Mrs Davis was in hospital, and any of the neighbours knew about it – which, judging by gossip prevalent at the time, some did – there could well have been quarrels once she returned home and discovered what was going on.

There was a perfectly plausible theory that on the morning of the murder, Davis had come home from his night shift and gone into Monica's bedroom. A suspicious Wilhelmina had caught them *in flagrante delicto*, and that he struck her, probably with the hammer which he had been using at work. It may have been an impulsive attack in a fit of temper; it may have been planned in order to dispose of the wife whom he had long since disliked and despised, and wished to eliminate so he could live in sin with Monica afterwards. He had not bargained for Monica becoming hysterical and frightened at the sight of her aunt lying dead in front of them. She started screaming, and in order to save his skin he had to silence her as well. They would then 'disappear' in the garage pit.

That his mental condition was in some doubt at the time would help to explain if not excuse his behaviour. It was noticed by the police that though the clothes in which he wrapped them were stained with blood, he had made a thorough job of cleaning up the bedrooms so that they left no tell-tale signs of violent death.

Davis appeared at court at Camborne on 1 June, and over proceedings lasting two days he was formally charged with the murders, though he pleaded not guilty. Mr G.R. Paling, prosecuting, summarised the events from after the last time Mrs Davis was seen alive by neighbours on 20 April and her niece the following day. James Simpson testified to having been present after disturbing soil in the inspection pit, and Norah Rowe said that Davis had always been very fond of his two small children, as well as of his niece. Charles Pearce, foreman at the engineering works, called Davis 'a quiet fellow, not exactly morose, but not cheerful', and had seen how upset he was at the death of his children.

He was then taken to Exeter Gaol to await the trial at Bodmin Assizes on 15 June before Mr Justice Lawrence. Mr G. Roberts opened the case for the prosecution, stating that on the night of 21 April or the next morning, the prisoner killed both women, by rendering them unconscious, and then asphyxiating them by tying something over their heads, then tried to conceal all evidence of the crime. The ten minutes on the evening of 27 April, when he said he was going to the Tuckingmill Hotel, were most likely the occasion when he moved the bodies from the house to the pit. He must have forced his way into the Simpson household in order to prevent Mrs Simpson from entering his home and making the ghastly discovery herself.

The first witness to give evidence was Norah Rowe. Almost at once she collapsed and fainted under the strain, and had to be revived with a glass of water. Out of sympathy for her – as she had suffered more than anybody else in the tragedy – the local press withheld her name in their reporting of the proceedings, though to anybody who had followed the case from the start, it must have been apparent who was being referred to. Among the other witnesses, Gladys Mitchell, a former assistant in Mr Andrew's shop, said she last saw Monica Rowe at about 4.30 p.m. on Wednesday 21 April, when she went in to buy some groceries. She was probably the last person outside the family to see the girl alive. Sergeant Stone said he had known Mr and Mrs Davis when they lived at Hayle, and thought they were happy enough on the whole. Nevertheless she did call on him once and ask what she needed to do if her husband should walk out on her and leave her penniless.

Mr Andrew also took the witness box, to describe his examination of the inspection pit and finding of the bodies. When questioned by Mr Brooks if there

The pit in the garage where Philip Davis's victims were discovered. (© Devon & Cornwall Constabulary)

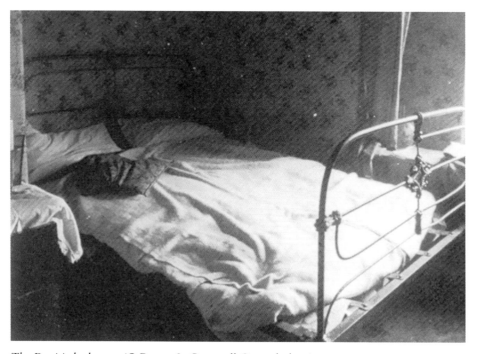

The Davis's bedroom. (© Devon & Cornwall Constabulary)

was any attempt to conceal the bodies, he said the prisoner had not been very skilful, and it was not 'a very workmanlike job'.

For the defence, Mr Lhind Pratt argued that the prisoner was not necessarily sane at the time he committed the murders. The evidence that they died at his hands rested on his confession. Could they rely on these confessions?

Alfred Davis, the accused's father, a labourer from Northampton, who had not seen his son for eleven years, told the court of his son's early years. Philip, said his father, was the eldest of five children by his first wife. She had become increasingly violent and obsessive after the births of each child, and after the last one appeared, she spent some time in a mental institution. Her father had also been notorious for his strange behaviour and violent temper. Alfred Davis's first wife had died in 1922 and he remarried five months later. The appearance of Martha, his stepmother, upset the nineteen-year-old Philip considerably. In February 1924 he found a job as a hallboy, but after six months he was brought home by the butler and a footman 'in a confused and rambling state'. He was locked in the bedroom, but proceeded to smash the furniture and break the lock on the door. The next day his father took him to Berry Wood Mental Hospital, Northampton, where he was certified insane, but after four months he was considered perfectly fit and discharged. His stepmother particularly dreaded him coming back home, and must have been very relieved when he joined the army in February 1925.

Unhappily, mental instability in the family did not stop there, for when Philip Davis came to trial at Bodmin twelve years later, his youngest brother was also confined in a similar institution.

The deputy superintendent of the Northampton hospital had checked Davis's records, and seen him just before the trial. He believed that the prisoner was suffering from dementia praecox, or schizophrenia, of a kind which often appeared during puberty and which could recur after periods of normality. Davis had recently become a patient of Dr Richard Henry Blair, and noted that according to the records, the doctor who had certified him insane had done so on account of his rambling talk, strange behaviour and regular attempts to interfere with his stepmother. Davis had accused the butler of molesting him, had deep-seated feelings of unworthiness and guilt, and a guilt complex after having started smoking at the age of thirteen. All this, the doctor said, was consistent with dementia praecox.

When cross-examined by Mr Roberts, Dr Blair said it would be his duty to certify Davis as insane. Health factors, financial problems, and the loss of both children within a short space of time could have contributed to a recurrence of mental illness, and that he would not have known what he was doing at the time that he attacked both women. When Roberts tried to harry Dr Blair regarding certification of the patient, suggesting he had reached this conclusion too quickly, Dr Blair stood firm, also citing Davis's lack of any show of emotion as an additional indication of his condition.

Dr Joshua Carse, deputy superintendent at Berrywood Mental Hospital, made it clear that in his view the background hereditary details in this case were important. There was a history of mental instability in the family, and the prisoner had been relapsing since December, culminating in an attack of complete confusion. Davis would not have been fully responsible for his actions when he attacked his wife and niece. Moreover he had had delusions of persecution, especially involving his neighbours, and should be certified as insane.

Others begged to differ. Roberts called three additional witnesses for the prosecution, the first being Mr Palmer from Hayle, who said he had known the prisoner for about five years, and never noticed anything abnormal about him. Dr Hugh Griersen, senior mental practitioner at Brixton Prison, who had interviewed Davis twice at Exeter Prison, found him to be quite rational in conversation, and normal in his conduct, while Dr Trevor Preece, the medical officer at Exeter Prison, had told him that Davis had not shown any evidence of mental disorder. In his final submission, Roberts reminded the jury that when the murder victims were found, Davis said, 'I was in a mental home. That is my only chance.' The one thought in his mind was to go back to the time when he was in a mental home, and would try and build a defence of insanity in order to avoid the full penalty of the law.

The judge took fifty minutes in his summing up. The jury was out for thirty-five minutes, and delivered a verdict of guilty. Davis appealed against the death sentence, and the case was heard again at the Court of Criminal Appeal on 12 July but dismissed. He was hanged on 27 July at Exeter Gaol by Thomas Pierrepoint and Thomas Phillips.

21

MURDER ON CHRISTMAS EVE

Falmouth, 1942

When Albert James Bateman was in his mid-fifties he retired from his profession as an accountant and took over a tobacconist's shop at Commercial Chambers, Arwenack Street, Falmouth. As the site was close to the harbour and docks, business was generally brisk. Every weekday he opened punctually at 9 a.m. and always stayed open throughout the lunch hour, until 2.30 p.m. so the dockyard workers would be able to call in during their break. After this he returned home, to Winnots, Fox's Lane, for lunch, returning to the shop at 3.30 p.m., sometimes accompanied by his wife as an assistant. He usually closed at around 5.30 p.m., leaving the premises about twenty minutes later so he would be home to hear the 6 p.m. news on the radio at home.

In 1942 he was aged sixty-one but he had always kept himself in good health, remaining fit through his regime of daily exercise.

On Christmas Eve trade was good, as was to be expected before the festive break. He was too busy to go home for lunch, so his wife took him some sandwiches. As he did not return home at his usual time in the early evening, she assumed at first that he had been deluged with customers and might have stayed open late in order to avoid disappointing anyone. However, when there was no sign of him by 7.30 p.m. she was concerned that something had gone wrong. She went to the shop and found it closed, locked and unlit. Her husband, she decided and hoped, must have gone home by another route, so she went back – only to find he had still not arrived. She collected a set of duplicate keys and walked back to the shop, but still there was no sign of light or any activity. Getting more worried by the minute, she ran down the street to get help, and soon found two policemen, Sergeant Bennetts and Constable (War Reserve) Drummond.

They entered the shop together about 8.30 p.m., and found it in total darkness. Although blackout time was around 5.45 p.m. – about the time he normally left to come home – the curtains had not been drawn. Sergeant Bennetts switched on his torch, and at once they saw the body of Albert Bateman lying in a pool of blood around his head, on the floor behind the counter. He was fully clothed, wearing his overcoat, and his face had been badly battered. It was assumed that he had been attacked as he was about to lock up and leave. Dr Dudley Harris was summoned to examine the body, and confirmed that he had been dead for around two hours.

Arwenack Street, Falmouth.
(© Kim Van der Kiste)

Across an inner passage from the shop was a tailor and outfitter where Phyllis Cooper worked as an assistant. She said that it had been part of Mr Bateman's usual routine to come out of the shop, pick up the doormat from outside his front door and take it to a cupboard under the stairs, then bang the door to and leave it locked. He would then return to the shop, put on his overcoat, change his cap for a trilby hat and set out for home. On the night he was killed, she heard all these things happen as usual, and assumed that he had gone home. Unfortunately, on this occasion he must have been confronted by an intruder as he was about to leave.

Superintendent Thomas Morcumb, head of the Falmouth Police Division, was sent for, and he contacted the pathologist Dr Hocking. After a preliminary examination of the body they took it to the Falmouth public mortuary for the post-mortem. This revealed evidence of asphyxiation, with several injuries to the face and head. There were bruises on the point of the chin, and over the larynx or Adam's apple. The left cheek was heavily bruised, and the upper jawbone underneath had been fractured. The lips were split, as was the skin over the left eyelid. The skull had been fractured at the back, and there was a large associated bruise in the scalp, and mottled bruising of the brain. The upper and lower dentures were smashed into several fragments, two lying on the floor of the shop near the head, the others embedded in blood clots at the back of the mouth. A

The body of Alfred Bateman behind his shop counter.
(© Devon & Cornwall Constabulary)

considerable quantity of blood had run down the air passages into the lungs, and these passages were completely obstructed.

Death had been caused by suffocation due to the inhalation of blood from injuries to the mouth and face while lying unconscious as a result of blows to the head, causing concussion. Two or more heavy blows had been struck on the face, one on the chin, the other on the left cheek. The fracture of the skull and damage to the brain might have been caused by Mr Bateman falling backwards after having been struck in the face, or possibly by contact with the wall or shelving behind him, as a result of blows to the face. It was also possible that some of the injury had been caused by stamping on the face, after falling. The blows could not have been self-inflicted, nor caused by any fall in the premises. There was no sign of any disturbance, and no sign of any blood on any object on to which the deceased might have accidentally fallen. The injuries and therefore death were due to assault. Temperature recordings confirmed that death had taken place at around 6 p.m. that evening.

An examination of the premises was carried out. The shop had not been ransacked, for £14 in notes was found on Mr Bateman, and almost £16 in silver and copper coins in an attaché case on a shelf behind a plywood screen. On the counter, in the till and various other places about seven shillings was recovered. Mrs Bateman said that at least £25 was missing. The crime, therefore, had probably been committed in the course of robbery, and the assailant must have known something of the habits of his intended victim, waiting until he disappeared into the back premises of his shop to lock up. He then ran into the shop, took what money was in the till, but as he tried to leave he was confronted by the tobacconist on his return from shutting up before he could get away.

Most significantly, on the counter was a bloodstained handkerchief, which Mrs Bateman recognised as having belonged to her husband. When taken for examination, it was proved that the blood on it was from his group, and it would appear that he had taken it out to staunch blood running from his face as a result of the first blow. Beside it was a 0.55 Mark II Webley revolver. At the request of Dr Harris he picked it up and broke it. All the chambers and the barrel were empty, and no expended cartridges were found nearby. Mrs Bateman said she had never seen it before. It had not been fired shortly before its discovery, as there was no lingering smell of cordite or gunpowder. It had been left behind by the assailant, who had entered the shop with it, probably in order to frighten and hold up the shopkeeper for money. Not finding him there he had put the weapon down, helped himself to what was in the till, then attacked the hapless shopkeeper who had just surprised him, and fled in panic – leaving the gun behind. It was packed up and taken to Scotland Yard to be examined for fingerprints, but none could be identified apart from those who had handled it since its discovery in the shop.

The gun, stamped with the number 33748, proved to be a crucial exhibit. On the outbreak of war in 1939 Falmouth Docks had been taken over by the Admiralty. The armed forces had commandeered some civilian equipment, including a 130-ton yacht *Ceto*, which had been converted into a compass calibrating vessel and thus become HM yacht *Ceto*. She was armed rather sparsely with three Lewis guns, four rifles, and a Webley service revolver – No. 33748.

Superintendent Morcumb recalled that some ten months earlier, a docks employee had reported the revolver as missing. All the arms had been removed from the *Ceto* to ammunition stores at the docks, lifted by crane and loaded into a Royal Naval covered truck just before dinnertime on 27 February 1942. The storehouseman reported that when he returned to the store at about 12.30 p.m. he saw that the weapons had been deposited in one particular store. He checked them, and noticed that although the canvas bag in which he had placed the weapon was still there, the revolver was missing. Several people who had been involved in the moving of weapons were interviewed, but without any results.

However one of the other dock labourers, Gordon Horace Trenoweth, who had unloaded the crane, had a police record after being sentenced for larceny in his youth. Aged thirty-three, he was married with five children. His wife had been in a mental institution since January 1941. When he found out that she was working there, as opposed to being a helpless patient unable to do anything for herself let alone for other people, he decided that she must be earning her keep and therefore refused to contribute anything towards her maintenance. For this he was sent to prison and released in November that year, after which he had gone back to live with his parents at Mallin's Cottage, High Street, Falmouth. When the weapon was reported missing he had allowed the police to come and search his home, and they found nothing incriminating.

The Webley revolver, left behind in Albert Bateman's shop after he had been killed.
(© Devon & Cornwall Constabulary)

Even so, Morcumb had not forgotten the incident, and decided that it might be well worth their while to interview Trenoweth again. At 3.45 a.m. on Christmas Day, he and Inspector Martin went to Mallin's Cottage. They found Trenoweth in bed; alongside him was a suit of clothes and a pair of brown shoes. When they examined the suit they noticed what seemed to be bloodstains on the right sleeve, and specks of blood on the shoes. He was detained and taken to the police station for questioning, where he was asked to account for his movements the previous afternoon and evening. He said he had been out shopping in the afternoon, before taking the 7 p.m. bus to Truro. Two packets of Woodbine cigarettes were found on him. When offered a Players cigarette by his visitors, he said he preferred Woodbines. Asked where he had bought those found on him, he told them they came from Reginald Pearce's in the high street. When questioned later neither Pearce nor his daughter, who had been working behind the shop counter, could recall having seen Trenoweth recently.

Trenoweth was told that a man had been found with severe facial injuries, and made the statement which probably did as much as anything else to put him in the dock. 'I bought the cigarettes at Pearce's,' he insisted, 'I was not in that man's shop.' How did he know who 'that man' was? When asked to account for the cash in his possession, a little over £5, he said, 'I don't want to say anything about the money.' As for the blood on his clothes, he told them it must have come from a nosebleed.

When Dr Hocking arrived at the police station on Christmas morning he examined Trenoweth, and found no sign of any recent nosebleed. He carried out tests on the hands with chemical reagents to indicate the probable presence of blood, and traced some on the back of the right hand and at the side of the nail of his third finger.

At this stage, Morcumb told Hocking that Bateman had been found dead in his shop at Falmouth with facial injuries, and that the detained man had failed to account for the blood on his clothes, or for his whereabouts on the previous evening, or indeed for the money found on him. At about 10 p.m. on what must surely have been the least pleasant Christmas Day any of those involved had ever known, Morcumb charged Trenoweth with the wilful murder of Albert James Bateman. His jacket, waistcoat, trousers and a shirt were handed over to Hocking, as well as the Webley revolver. The pathologist noted that on the right cuff of the shirt was a mark which looked like a washed-out bloodstain. Later laboratory tests showed that it was indeed human blood. Similar stains were found on the suit on the right cuff of the jacket, seven circular drops, up to quarter of an inch in diameter, and a small drop on the middle button of the waistcoat.

The suit was of good quality, and the good state of the trouser pocket linings suggested that the garment had not been heavily worn. However, at the bottom of the left trouser pocket was a tear about two and a half inches long. The hole had been torn by the Webley revolver. Hocking suspected that the weapon, about a foot in length, would be extremely obvious if placed in a trouser pocket. The accused must have carried it around with him, concealed in the pocket, probably as he was walking around the shopping centre of Falmouth on the day before, planning to intimidate some shopkeeper into handing him the savings. This would also explain why no fingerprints were found on the gun, as they would have been rubbed off while Trenoweth was out walking.

An inquest was opened on 28 December by the Coroner, Mr Carlyon. Mrs Bateman gave evidence of identification of her husband, Dr Hocking described the injuries in detail, and Superintendent Morcumb gave an account of events. Trenoweth was remanded in custody for twenty-one days, and the Coroner adjourned the inquiry until the conclusion of criminal proceedings.

Later, Hocking and Inspector Martin went to Trenoweth's home to investigate the possibility that the revolver, missing from *Ceto* for nearly a year, may have been in his possession all that time. Mallin's Cottage, they discovered, faced the waterfront of the Fal estuary, and was approached down a narrow passageway where in sailing ship times men and youths were shanghaied for service at sea. The upper part of the house was a large sail and spar storing loft, and when entered seemed to be full of the unwanted junk of generations. They searched carefully among this material, and found a strip of multicoloured carpet. Brushings from the carpet examined through a microscope showed the presence of all the hairs, cotton and wood fibres, and miscellaneous objects such as black horsehair and portions of feather, which an examination of the revolver and trouser pockets had revealed.

All this was almost enough to condemn Trenoweth. One more piece of evidence proved his guilt beyond a shadow of a doubt. When he was first interviewed at his home, his clothing was searched, and when the money was checked, four £1 notes were found. One of these notes, numbered H 59D 650932, was torn on one corner and carefully repaired with a strip of white paper. The ever-organised Mr Bateman was known to be very careful about repairing torn banknotes, and had sometimes been seen in his shop doing so. Early on the day of the murder, a Mr Sowden had called in the shop and noticed him engaged thus. On 31 December, Sergeant Bennetts and Detective Constable Eden searched Mr Bateman's shop and sorted through all the waste paper they could find. Eventually they came across a crumpled bill head with a corner cut out, and when they matched it with the stolen note, they found the missing corner matched the repair exactly. The note, gum and cut bill head were sent to the Forensic Laboratory at Bristol, and the Director, Mr Parkes, confirmed that the gum on the note and bill head were identical in composition.

Trenoweth was charged with murder at Exeter Assizes on 11 February 1943, presided over by Mr Justice Tucker, and the trial lasted for five days. On the first day, after giving evidence, Mrs Bateman collapsed and had to be carried out of court. Dr Harris confirmed that Mr Bateman was dead when he examined the body. The tobacconist had been a patient of his, and was treated for occasional injuries to wrist and knee, but had otherwise been in good health.

The evidence with regard to the revolver and the pound note was overwhelming. The Woodbine cigarettes found on Trenoweth when he was arrested, and other packets of the same brand, were also sent to Mr Parkes at Bristol. He proved that the cigarettes in the prisoner's possession had been part of a delivery made to Mr Bateman, and to nobody else in Falmouth. In the end this was not used in court, as the other evidence was considered proof enough.

For the prosecution, led by Mr J.D. Caswell, the court had the evidence of Dorothy Allen whom he had met in Truro, later on Christmas Eve. She said that they had arranged to meet in Truro on Christmas Eve and he was late for the appointment; he had missed the 6.15 p.m. bus, but caught the next one at 7 p.m. When they went to the Market Tavern, Gordon was being quite lavish with his money that night for an unemployed man usually short of money. On this occasion he paid for drinks for her, two for her mother, and one each for two soldiers, in addition to his own. Before he left he said he was going to buy her a new pair of shoes, but she said she would rather have the money instead, so he gave her a £1 note. His spending at the bar was confirmed by the barman, Frederick Griffiths. The cash had almost certainly come from Bateman's shop.

Mr J. Scott Henderson, Counsel for the Defence, suggested that Trenoweth could have picked up the banknote from the shop in the course of other

A £1 note repaired by Albert Bateman and found in Gordon Trenoweth's pockets when he was searched on Christmas Day. (© Devon & Cornwall Constabulary)

transactions during the day, but to no avail. The likelihood of his having done so was very remote.

On the last day of the trial, Trenoweth told the court that he spent much of Christmas Eve looking for work. As there was none to be had at the docks, he visited the Employment Exchange. He bought two packets of cigarettes at Pearce's shop, and had several drinks. Instead of going home for dinner he bought himself a pasty, then in the afternoon 'patrolled around the shops'. At 5.30 p.m. he went to Messrs Harris's coalyard, looking for work, and spoke to Harry Osberg, the managing clerk. He arrived home for tea about 5.40 p.m., a fact readily confirmed by his father Gordon, saw his parents and children, and read the newspaper for half an hour. He asked them the time, was told it was 6.35 p.m., as his sister Mona, a cinema usherette, confirmed. Leaving to check on the time of the next bus to Truro, he then visited the pub before catching the 7 p.m. to Truro. He stayed at the Market Inn with Dorothy Allen for about two hours, caught the 9.30 p.m. bus back to Falmouth, returned home about 10.15 p.m. and was in bed by 11 p.m.

'What did you think the police came to your house about?', Henderson asked him.

'About the maintenance,' he answered.

'Was there any reason why they should get you out of bed in the middle of the night?'

'Not that I know of.'

The jury found Trenoweth guilty, 'but with a strong recommendation to mercy, as it is not considered the accused intended to kill.' He showed no emotion, and remained silent when Mr Justice Tucker asked if he had anything to say as to why he should not be sentenced to death. The judge said he would forward the recommendation to the proper quarter. Nevertheless the Court of Appeal saw no reason to intervene, and on 6 April 1943 Trenoweth went to the gallows, his executioners being Thomas Pierrepoint and Herbert Morris. He was the last man to be hanged at Exeter Gaol.

Writing his memoirs some years later, Dr Hocking said he was sure Trenoweth did not have murder in mind when he was caught with his hands in the till, believed the sentence was too severe for the crime, and thought him unlucky to have done so at a time when the law was administered 'with much more harshness'. The Court of Appeal took the not unnatural view that Mr and Mrs Bateman were the really unlucky ones, particularly at what should have been the season of peace and goodwill to all mankind.

22

'PLEASE, DON'T LET US THINK OF SATURDAY'

Lizard Point, 1943

The possibility of an early death at the hands of the enemy was all too realistic for British fighting forces during the Second World War. Hence, whenever they got the chance in those uncertain times, young people tended to live for the moment and seize any opportunity for pleasure. The troops stationed in Cornwall during the hostilities were no exception to the rule. Those who counted themselves particularly fortunate were the young men and women stationed at the RAF base near Lizard Point, since they were billeted in a commandeered luxury hotel. The Housel Bay Hotel, set high on the cliffs of the rugged Cornish coast, is said to be the most southerly hotel in Britain and the servicemen and women staying there enjoyed many a party on the beach below.

Housel Bay Hotel, The Lizard.

Housel Bay and Lizard lighthouse.

Corporal Joan Lewis, aged twenty-seven, a WAAF from Porthcawl, had been at Housel Bay for some time before the arrival of a new station commander, Flying Officer William Croft from Bath, who was five years older. The couple first met at a beach party and, thrown together by their work, their initial friendship soon deepened into a passionate affair.

Their relationship troubled Croft, a married man with two children. He was not just committing adultery, but also engaging in fraternisation between the ranks, a practice very much frowned upon by the armed forces. At length his guilty conscience prompted him to confide in Freda Catlin, the officer who was in charge of the WAAFs. Catlin advised him in no uncertain terms that the affair should stop immediately, since it was not conducive to either morale or discipline. Not only must the association cease, but one of the lovers must be reposted.

Croft's application for a transfer was refused, so arrangements were made for Joan Lewis to be moved to another station in Devon on Saturday 16 October 1943. Once her move had been organised, Croft found that he could hardly bear the prospect of being parted from her. In one of the many love letters to pass between the couple, Croft wrote: 'The thought of some other male sharing your company drives me to distraction. Please, don't let us think of Saturday, Joan darling. I cannot dare to think of it. Every time, I get a horrible aching pain.'

Joan was permitted a couple of days leave before her transfer, which she spent with Croft, before returning to duty on 14 October. On the following day, she seemed quite cheerful, if resigned, and the couple spent that night together in a summerhouse in the hotel garden. Towards dawn, the noise of two shots was heard coming from the summerhouse. Seconds later, Croft ran to the hotel where he approached the Duty Officer and told him that he had killed Joan. He later telephoned another officer and begged him to come to the summerhouse immediately. In the course of the call Croft was heard to say; 'I have killed Joan Lewis' and 'I have shot Joan.'

The summer house at Housel Bay Hotel. (© Devon & Cornwall Constabulary)

Interior of the summer house. (© Devon & Cornwall Constabulary)

Flying Officer Norman Page and a sergeant rushed to the summerhouse. Climbing through the window, they discovered the body of Joan Lewis, which had apparently fallen from a sofa and lay in a pool of blood on the floor. On a table, near to the body, they saw a Webley service revolver, later found to contain two empty cartridges and four live rounds of ammunition. The firing pin had struck a third bullet, which had not fired.

Croft asked the officers to inform the police, explaining that, in desperation at being parted, he and Lewis had made a suicide pact. Joan had, he maintained, fired both shots. He had been supposed to shoot himself with the same revolver, but had not had the courage to go through with it.

Police Superintendent Thomas Morcumb arrived at the hotel at about 7 a.m., accompanied by Dr Hocking. There, in the summerhouse, they completed a preliminary examination of Lewis' body, concluding that she had been shot twice, once in the chest and once in the head.

Joan's body was removed to the RAF headquarters at nearby Predannack, where Hocking was able to conduct a full post-mortem. He found that Joan had first been shot in the chest, the shot probably aimed at her heart, but missing by some five or six inches. The bullet had struck a rib and then deviated upwards and backwards, exiting via the woman's armpit, damaging the left lung and also the musculature used in raising the arm. This shot had been fired while she was sitting on the sofa and a bloodstained hole was found in the sofa back, from which a flattened bullet was subsequently removed. The second shot had been the fatal one, entering the skull just above and behind the left eye and exiting behind the right ear.

Croft was charged with the murder of Joan Lewis at Helston Police Court on 16 November. Despite having been clearly heard admitting to shooting and killing Joan, Croft now stuck to his revised story of a suicide pact between them, saying 'At this stage all I wish to say is that I did not murder Joan Lewis. She shot herself twice. We had both agreed to commit suicide.' He said that the pair had woken in the summerhouse at about 4.30 a.m. on a rainy, windy morning, on which the moon was obscured by clouds. Having spent their time together talking, smoking and dozing, Croft now placed the gun on his lap and the pair agreed that whoever felt like making the first move would use the gun, leaving the survivor to follow. According to his confession, Croft fell asleep again, to be awakened by a loud bang.

He saw Joan clasping her chest, complaining of pain and begging him to go and get help, at which he climbed out of the window and ran towards the hotel. He had no sooner set off, than he heard the second shot. Rushing back to the summerhouse, he snatched up the revolver and put it to his own head, but was unable to fire.

Mr E.G. Robey, prosecuting, said that a number of letters had passed between Croft and Lewis, and letters in the possession of the prosecution clearly indicated the state of mind of both before 16 October. 'They will show you he was a man obviously very jealous, very much in love with this girl and she with him; a man who was married and thought of his marriage as an obstacle which seemed to worry him much. They were both obviously dreading the separation.' He claimed that it was quite impossible for Lewis to have shot herself.

Croft went on trial for the murder of Joan Lewis at the Winchester Assizes on 14 December 1943, before Mr Justice Humphreys. Throughout the trial the defence maintained that Lewis had fired the shots, as part of a suicide pact. However, the prosecution insisted that this was impossible, calling Hocking as an expert witness. Hocking put himself through a number of contortions in the witness box to demonstrate to the jury the difficulties that Joan would have faced in firing both shots herself.

He conceded that Joan could possibly have fired the first shot, although he felt that this was unlikely. For a start, the gun was heavy and required a trigger pressure of almost seven pounds when cocked and eighteen pounds when uncocked to discharge it. The degree of burning on the front of Lewis' uniform tunic indicated that the gun had been about five inches away from the body when fired. Hocking maintained that, to fire the gun from this position. Joan would have been forced to pull the trigger with her thumb, an awkward and unlikely occurrence.

However Hocking was adamant that Lewis could not have fired the second, fatal shot to the head herself. The first shot had so damaged the muscles on the front of her chest that it would have been impossible for her to raise the heavy gun, hold it a distance of twelve to eighteen inches from her head and pull the trigger with her thumb. The final placement of the gun was also a consideration. Hocking felt that the awkward position in which the gun was held for the first shot, would have caused it to fly uncontrollably from Lewis' hand, had she been the one to pull the trigger. It seemed beyond belief that, bleeding heavily and in severe pain, she had then scrabbled about in the dark summerhouse to find the weapon, before cocking it and firing the second shot.

In summing up the case for the jury, the judge outlined the finer points of the law on suicide. It was, he explained, self-murder and, if Lewis had indeed committed suicide, as the prosecution maintained, then she was guilty of murder. At the same time, if Croft had in any way aided and abetted the suicide, he was as guilty of murder as if he had shot her himself.

The jury debated for less than twenty minutes before finding William Croft guilty of the murder of Joan Lewis and he was sentenced to hang. Almost immediately, the case was sent to the Court of Criminal Appeal on the grounds of misdirection by the judge.

It was argued that the judge had neglected to mention the possibility that Lewis' death may have been accidental. The prosecution had suggested that, having fired the first shot, Joan's hand or elbow might have violently struck the table near to the sofa, causing the gun to fire again, resulting in the fatal shot to the head. In addition, if the second shot had, as Croft contended, been fired by Joan while he was on his way to summon help, then he could hardly have been accused of counselling, procuring, advising or abetting suicide, since he was not present when the fatality occurred.

In taking the loaded revolver to the summerhouse, Croft had clearly provided the means for Joan Lewis to commit suicide, if indeed his story of a mutual pact were true. And, in leaving the summerhouse to seek help, he had undoubtedly left a severely wounded woman alone with a loaded revolver, rather than trying to offer first aid or removing the revolver from the scene to prevent further injury. And, if Joan had actually asked him to seek help, did that not indicate a wish to live, so negating any suicide pact?

After much legal wrangling, including a hearing at the Court of Criminal Appeal on 21 January 1944, Croft's appeal was dismissed. His sentence was however reduced from the death penalty to life imprisonment and, in the event, he was released from prison only a few years later.

The case of Croft and Lewis still holds many mysteries and Hocking, in *Bodies and Crimes* (1992), outlines further evidence, which was not presented to the jury in the original trial. It was mentioned that the pistol contained a further four live bullets, in addition to the two that had been discharged in the course of the fatal shooting. Hocking points out that five of the six cartridges in the weapon were 0.455 inches in diameter – the sixth, was a smaller cartridge, measuring 0.450 inches, intended for use in a Smith and Wesson revolver, which was also common

An artist's impression of the ghost of Joan Lewis. (© Devon & Cornwall Constabulary)

military issue at the time. It was this smaller cartridge that showed evidence of being struck twice by the firing pin, but because of its size, it had slipped slightly in the cylinder. Thus, the impact of the firing pin was lessened, with the result that the gun did not fire.

Hocking cites this as evidence of confirmation of a suicide pact between Croft and Lewis, in that Croft may have tried unsuccessfully to kill himself, before leaving Joan to seek help. However it does not alter the fact that it was Croft who pulled the trigger, if not twice, then at least for the fatal head shot. In Hocking's opinion, the tragic death of Joan Lewis was indeed the result of a suicide pact that went wrong.

And, it appears that this opinion may even have been confirmed from beyond the grave! Several seemingly reliable witnesses, with no prior knowledge of the tragedy, have reported seeing a young woman sitting on a bench in the gardens of the Housel Bay Hotel. The woman, whose physical description tallies closely with that of Joan Lewis, wears a WAAF uniform and is always reported as either looking sad, or weeping. One witness, who was a spiritual medium, even managed to engage the young woman in 'conversation'. The medium was told that the young WAAF was waiting for her lover – who was also her murderer – to join her, as he had promised in a suicide pact, in 1943.

In recent years, there have been no further reported sightings of the ethereal woman on the bench. Is it possible that, so many years after her murder, she has finally been joined by her lover and is now able to rest in peace?

23

'I HAVE HAD A TERRIBLE ROW WITH THE OLD MAN'

St Austell, 1952

On 7 August 1923 Charles Giffard married Elizabeth Goodwin at the Church of St Mary's, Rockbeare, near Exeter. His family came from Englefield Green, Surrey, and while she was Irish by birth, previously her parents had moved to the Westcountry. They made their home in Cornwall, and to all outward appearances were a happy, well-to-do family. Charles, or 'Charlie' to his friends, had served with the Royal Flying Corps towards the end of the First World War, and became Commandant of the Special Constabulary in the St Austell Division during the Second World War. He was the senior partner in a firm of solicitors, was later made Clerk to the Social Justices with particular responsibility for advising on sentences, and also an Under Sheriff of Cornwall. During his leisure time he was often to be found in the club or his local, the White Hart, St Austell. He had a favourite registration number, ERL 1, which he transferred from one car to the next. Elizabeth, the elder by three years, was Vice-Chairman of the St Austell Conservative Association and President of the Conservative Women's Association, and played bridge two or three times a week with her friends.

At first they settled in the parish of St Mewan. A few years later they had their own house built on the cliff top at Porthpean, overlooking St Austell Bay, and about two miles from the town. Carrickowl, an imposing residence, tended to overawe visitors, with its fishing rods and golf clubs in the hall, a large breakfast room with dishes and hot plates on the sideboard.

Elizabeth was much liked in the community, but the same could not be said of her husband who was known as a hard, unsympathetic man, overbearing and brusque, never one to suffer fools gladly. Their elder son Miles found it hard to live up to the exacting standards of two such pillars of the community, especially in view of his history of instability, bordering on mental illness.

Miles was born in 1926, and his brother Robin about three years later. Both used to play together around the cliffs and in the woodland nearby. Miles often had nightmares as a child. When he was about two he had a nanny who beat

Porthpean, near St Austell.

him and often locked him in a dark cupboard for punishment. When this was discovered she was dismissed for cruelty, but the psychological damage to the boy had already been done. During his adolescence he was often punished for lying and stealing his mother's jewellery, though she always stood up for him. At the age of thirteen he was sent to Rugby public school where he was hopelessly dirty and untidy, still an incorrigible liar, wet the bed, and screwed up his sheets with his hands, then bit holes in them, an inch or two in diameter. After four terms the masters found him impossible. There were consultations between Mr and Mrs Giffard and the headmaster and he was removed from the school. It was the worst possible time for the family as his father was then in the throes of a nervous breakdown, probably as a result of his taking on too many cases for absent colleagues during the war years and driving himself too hard.

At the age of fourteen Miles was sent home and an appointment was made for him to see a Devon psychiatrist, Dr Roy Neville Craig. The doctor found Miles abnormally apathetic, dull and stupid. He had a psychopathic personality, was unresponsive to love and punishment and therefore impossible to control, so lacking in normal emotions that it was impossible to make him laugh or upset him. Adolescence had not lessened his tendency to lie or have nightmares, and there was now an alarming new development – panic attacks (or 'paroxysms of fear for no apparent reason') as well. Diagnosing his problems as a rare form of schizophrenia, implying that he had in effect lost touch with reality, the doctor treated him for two years, but was reluctant to give him any more than the most basic treatment, because of the risk that he might activate deep and violent disturbances in his mind. Nevertheless he warned Charles and Elizabeth of the possibility that their son could suffer a mental breakdown in the future.

The main buildings, Blundell's School, Tiverton. (From *The Blundellian*, 1932)

If another school was found for Miles where he could make a fresh start, Dr Craig hoped there was a chance that he might be able to develop more or less normally as long as he was treated with care. Craig used his influence to get him into Blundell's, a public school at Tiverton, far nearer to the Giffards' home than Rugby. He entered at the start of summer term 1941 and stayed until the end of autumn term 1943. At first arrangements were made for him to receive treatment three times a fortnight at school, but this meant he would miss games, the only thing at which he was any good. It must be assumed that they managed to treat him at different times instead, for denying Miles the chance to play cricket or other games would have been the worst punishment anybody could devise. Even so, his behaviour at Blundell's still gave cause for concern. One day he flew into a violent rage, stuck a knife into his leg, and then seemed surprised that it hurt and was bleeding. Nevertheless, though his academic achievements were negligible, he became a good sportsman. He played squash and excelled at cricket, playing for the school First XI in his final summer term. According to the school magazine, *The Blundellian*, in his last summer term, he evidently had good and bad cricket days;

> For one who gave such promise at the beginning, the season was a series of disasters relieved only by some good innings in house matches. The belief that he is full of runs still persists in spite of his failures and we think this belief justifiable. His fielding improved noticeably.

At one time Miles considered becoming a professional cricketer. His exacting, hard-to-please father dismissed the idea as absurd, and wanted him to become a solicitor. He sometimes spoke of his cricketing aspirations to Joan Baxter, landlady of his local, the Carlyon Arms at Sandy Bottom. She was a regular confidante of his, and he always struck her, she said, as 'a decent boy'. More than most others in the neighbourhood, she knew how much he loathed his father, with good reason. Chilly relations between both men became more distant still. To make matters worse, Robin was apparently an ideal son and never caused his parents any trouble at all. Elizabeth felt sorry for her unsatisfactory elder child, but maybe she found it difficult to conceal her preference for the second sibling.

Between 1943 and 1947 Miles did four years' National Service in the Royal Navy. On the lower deck this previously unstable and unhappy young adult suddenly came into his own. Though short he was strong and athletic, and the scapegoat, the useless child who could never live up to expectations, became a confident young man and an excellent sailor, well-mannered and liked by everyone. Far from resenting or railing against the ordered and disciplined conditions of service life, he adapted well. Being away from home, and particularly from his father, clearly did him a world of good. If he had chosen to remain in the Navy, tragedy might have been averted.

Unhappily for all concerned, afterwards Miles went back home. His time in the Navy had given him a greater degree of self-confidence. Until then he had probably assumed that his father was always right, and that if he was angry with him, he deserved it. Now perhaps he could see that his father was an authoritarian headstrong bully who would never admit he could be wrong. It was a view which many of Charles Giffard's peers shared.

Back at home Miles had a succession of poorly-paid jobs (including a boring unhappy spell in the family's solicitors' office), none of which he kept for long, and took to drinking more than was good for him. One day Charles lost patience with him, ordered him to leave the house and never darken his doors again. Miles accordingly left, but returned when the premises were empty and robbed them. Elizabeth persuaded her husband to forgive their prodigal son and let him back, and Charles agreed to give him one more chance. Miles came back and promised to give the office another try – until in November 1951 he inherited a legacy of £750 and went to live in Bournemouth.

Within four months he had spent the money, taken a few more dead-end jobs to support himself, including selling ice cream and working in an estate agent's office in Ringwood, then 'scrounged around' before returning home in June 1952 for want of any alternative. Two months later he went to London where he rented a furnished room at Walpole Street, Chelsea, soon exhausted the £15 monthly allowance from his father, then bounced cheques and borrowed money from friends.

During this time he met a girl of nineteen, Gabrielle Vallance, and her mother, who lived in Tite Street, Chelsea. They both took an instant liking to him, and he was totally smitten by Gabrielle. Intent on impressing her, he took her to shows and smart dining establishments around the West End, continuing to live well beyond his means. One day she took him gently to task about his untidy appearance, and as he could not afford any more clothes, he told her that his parents would send him some from Cornwall. As there was little prospect of his father going out of his way to help, he decided he would have to make a quick visit back.

He hitchhiked back to Cornwall, spending the night of Saturday 1 November in a rat-infested barn in Somerset, returning to Carrickowl the next day. He was optimistic that his father would produce some more money. But Charles Giffard did not approve of Gabrielle, and told Miles he wanted him to end the relationship. Maybe he thought Gabrielle was bad for his son; maybe he resented the fact that someone was about to have more influence on the young man than his parents, and he, Charles Giffard, successful solicitor and pillar of the establishment, did not intend to lose control. At the age of twenty-six, he went on, it was time Miles settled down, got out of the habit of spending more than he could afford, stayed in Cornwall, gave up all these fanciful ideas of playing sport for a career, and came to work in the family solicitors' office like his father.

Miles was horrified by the thought of losing Gabrielle, whom he had known for only six weeks yet hoped would be the love of his life. A sixteen-year-old schoolboy who lived nearby had been getting a little too friendly with her, and he dreaded leaving the way clear for his junior rival. At around this time he proposed to her, and she agreed to marry him, as long as he found a steady job first, preferably in London, so that he would be independent of his parents. If his father was going to stand between them, there was only one drastic solution.

On Monday 3 November he wrote to Gabrielle, telling her that what he was afraid would happen had come to pass;

> I have had a terrible row with the old man, made worse by the fact that, as usual, he is right. Anyway, the upshot of the whole thing is that he has forbidden me to return to London at any rate for the time being. He says he will cut me off without the proverbial penny, so there does not seem to be any alternative until I can get a job. I shall not be able to take you to Twickenham. Who will? I am terribly fed up and miserable as I was especially looking forward to seeing you tomorrow, and now God and the old man know when I shall. Short of doing him in, I see no future in the world at all. He has stopped my allowance, anyway, is giving me a pint of beer and 20 cigs a day, and has said, 'No Pubs'. No doubt your mother would approve. Give her my love and tell her that when she sees me I shall be a reformed character (nominally anyway).

Two days later he told her that he hoped to get to London that weekend after all, if he could talk his father round. How much he tried, if at all, and how Charles Giffard reacted, can only be guessed at. What is known for certain is that on the evening of 6 November Mrs Giffard went to her regular charity bridge drive in St Austell. She might have had car trouble, for on the morning of 7 November she took her husband's vehicle to attend a local Conservative branch meeting in Plymouth, while husband and son went to St Austell together in hers. Whether they went for any purpose other than getting the car fixed, or what conversation passed between them, is not recorded. They returned home for lunch, and Mr Giffard went back to his office that afternoon.

Left on his own in the house, Miles spent the next few hours curled up with a book about a jealous soldier who had murdered his girlfriend. At some stage during the afternoon or early evening he took four aspirins and knocked back half a bottle of whisky. This may have been before or after 5.30 p.m. when he rang Gabrielle, saying he intended to drive to London that night to do some business for his father. Two hours after this phone call his parents returned to the house in quick succession, in separate cars. His father was the first to arrive, and his mother followed a few minutes later, after taking a friend home.

Taking an iron pipe from the garden, Miles walked up to his father as he was getting out of the car and hit him. One blow missed and tore the lining of the door, but the others struck Charles on his hand, which he had thrown up to protect his face. Several more on the right side of the head knocked him unconscious. Mrs Giffard had gone indoors; she almost certainly had no idea what was going on, otherwise she would surely have tried to restrain her son. Miles then followed her in and struck her from behind until she was unconscious as well. He had probably not intended to kill his mother, who had always staunchly defended him as best she could from his father's tyrannical behaviour, but he could not avoid the risk of detection. If he had killed his father (who was still alive at the time), she would not have found assault with a heavy weapon as easy to forgive as persistent lying and theft. In a panic, he decided that she would also have to die.

Next he telephoned Gabrielle again to confirm that he would definitely come to London. Returning to the garage to fetch his father's car, he found Charles was coming round, and a few more blows with the bar killed him. Miles then went back to the kitchen, found his mother also recovering consciousness, and attacked her again. This time he did not succeed in despatching her, and he was concerned at the amount of blood around the house. After loading his still-breathing mother into a wheelbarrow, he took her to the edge of the cliff and pushed her over, then did the same with his father's corpse. It took him an hour to clean the house.

Barbara Orchard, the nineteen-year-old live-in housemaid at Carrickowl, had had a half-day and was expected back at any moment, so he did not want to leave any tell-tale signs. He finished his grisly tasks in time to throw a few things into his mother's car, including a change of clothes, his mother's jewellery which he had already stolen once before, and some sleeping pills which he later said he intended to take in order to commit suicide, then drove off shortly after 10 p.m. Miss Orchard had spent the afternoon with her fiancé, John Vaughan, who was bringing her back at the same time. She noticed Miles accidentally reversing into the house – the Triumph was notoriously difficult to manoeuvre, even if the driver was not intent on making a swift getaway – before driving off at high speed. In the weeks to come, did she ever realise that had she arrived a few minutes earlier, she might have met a similar violent death?

Miles changed his clothes en route, and threw some of the bloodstained garments into the river at Fenny Bridges. At the same time he disposed of the iron pipe, 2½ft long and 3lb in weight. Picking up two hitch-hikers near Ilchester, he took them to Chelsea. They noticed that he seemed a little tense and was chain-smoking throughout the drive, but seemed 'a very good sort of chap'.

He reached Tite Street at about 6 a.m. the following day, and slept in the car for a couple of hours before knocking on the door. In view of the physical efforts involved regarding his pushing a heavily-laden wheelbarrow twice some distance over rough ground late on a dark night, and the whisky he had consumed, combined with the complexity of a road journey from St Austell to London in the pre-motorway age, the overnight drive was no mean feat. He left the ignition key and some bloodstained shoes and clothing inside the vehicle, then spent about an hour with Gabrielle and Mrs Vallance, telling them that he had left his car at a garage and was staying with relatives at St John's Wood. He had a business appointment for 10 a.m., and would return for lunch. On leaving them he went to Piccadilly Circus and sold his mother's jewellery (not for the first time) for £50. Next he phoned Gabrielle to say he would not be able to make it back for lunch, but would meet her at 2 p.m. She came with her mother and all three went to see the Charlie Chaplin film *Limelight*, after which Mrs Vallance went home, leaving the young couple to their own devices.

Until then Miles had been unusually quiet, but a few drinks loosened his tongue. While they were drinking in the Star, Chesham Mews, he asked Gabrielle to marry him. She said yes, as long as he got a proper job first. Soon after this, he told her that he had done something frightful. 'What, pinched your father's car?' she asked. He replied that he had murdered his father and mother and would not be able to see her again. She realised he was upset about something, but she did not believe him, thinking he was trying to impress her and may also have been a little drunk. Perhaps she did not want to think that her boyfriend was capable of such a dreadful deed. They then went to another public house in the East End, the Prospect of Whitby beside the Thames at Wapping, for further refreshment. By the time he had summoned a taxi, they were both fairly tipsy. He was booked into the Regent Palace Hotel in the name of Gregory, and he gave her his room number, asking her to ring him early the next morning.

Meanwhile back in Cornwall, on returning to Carrickowl the previous (Friday) evening, Miss Orchard had not initially suspected anything wrong. Tired at the end of a long day, she had half-expected Mr and Mrs Giffard to be home, but as they sometimes stayed out late, their absence in itself gave no cause for alarm. At first she saw no reason to do a cursory check of the house indoors before going to bed. However, she noticed that the hall light was on, and then also found the garage light on. Entering the house, she noticed an outdoor coat and picnic basket which Mrs Giffard had taken with her to Plymouth that morning were lying on a kitchen chair, and her handbag and shoes were in the hall. She then noticed some coconut matting covering part of the floor had been removed, a rubber mat was damp, and there were smears on the floor, indicating that it had just been washed and probably in a hurry. Looking more closely, she saw what looked like bloodstains on the floor and cooker, and that a scrubbing brush, which was usually left outside the kitchen door, was still in the scullery sink.

Increasingly concerned that nobody was home, she rang two local hospitals to ask if they knew anything. As they did not, she sat down and considered the problem, then went to bed but not surprisingly had a sleepless night. After a few hours she could stand it no longer, so she got up and went to her fiancé's house at about 5 a.m. She told him of her discoveries and fears for the worst, in view of her employers being missing, that she had heard the larger car being driven away, and she was sure it must have been taken by the son of the house. That he was on the worst of terms with his father was no secret. Vaughan spoke to his gardener, Harry Launcelot Rowe, who promptly contacted the police, and then drove to Carrickowl to see for himself.

The message was passed on to Detective Superintendent Ken Julian of the Cornwall CID at his Bodmin headquarters. He and his Scene of Crimes Officer, PC Max Mutton, set out for the house, joined on their way by Dr Hocking, who was a family friend of the Giffards, Police Sergeant Lovering, and several other police officers. When they reached Carrickowl to join Rowe, tell-tale signs were evident. The earth floor of the garage and the interior and exterior of Mrs Giffard's car were covered with bloodstains; the other vehicle was missing. Another large stain outside the garage led to more of the same, together with a tuft of hair later identified as from the scalp of Mr Giffard, and marks on the garden path leading towards the gate suggesting that a heavily-laden wheelbarrow had been pushed that way. Further stains near the gate indicated that the barrow must have overturned at that point. A handkerchief heavily stained with blood was found just outside the gate, on top of the hedge. It had obviously been used by the person pushing the barrow to wipe his hands. Part of the wall at the rear of the house had been damaged and a car door handle lay nearby, bearing witness to Miles' hurried departure.

The trail of more of the same led them along a public footpath, beside the cliff top, and through a tangle of thorn bushes. At one point they found various articles including a wallet, a hat, a bunch of keys and a bundle of letters, most of which could be traced to the missing solicitor, a collection of loose coins, and a woman's hat, all stained with blood. The tracks took them across an area of ploughed land to the cliff edge. Below, on Duporth beach, they could see the sprawled body of a man lying on his back, with a wheelbarrow beside him. The top of his skull had been so badly damaged by the fall that his brains had splattered out over a rock.

At first they could see no sign of Mrs Giffard, and they suspected that her husband's killer might have taken her hostage. Then they saw more wheelbarrow tracks along the cliff path, and at one point, on the edge of a sheer drop, further bloodstains. Walking along the beach, they found her body about 200yds away from that of her husband, jammed face downwards between two rocks. When Dr Hocking examined her later, he decided that she had been knocked unconscious in the kitchen but was still alive when she was thrown over the cliff, and that she must have died when her head struck the rocks. She had two large bruises in her scalp, which had been split, with extensive injuries which had been caused about the time of her death, when her body was flung over the cliff and by sliding down the rough edge. The tide was within a few feet of the foot of the cliff, and under normal conditions a body thrown from the top would have been washed out to sea before long. It was unfortunate for Miles Giffard that the weather had been unusually mild at the time.

None of the men doubted for a moment who they were looking for in connection with the crimes. A general alert was sent out to all police stations, and within hours the missing Triumph, with its distinctive number plate ERL 1, was tracked down in Tite Street. Shortly after 11 p.m. on the Saturday night a taxi drew up outside the front door of No. 40, and a girl – Gabrielle Vallance – climbed out. As the taxi moved away police cars hedged it in, and plain clothes officers wrenched open the door. They had done so with some trepidation, as a search of Carrickowl revealed no sign of his father's revolver, and they thought

The footpath leading to Porthpean, along which Miles Giffard pushed the wheelbarrow containing his parents' bodies. (© Devon & Cornwall Constabulary)

Miles might have taken it with him. Their anxieties were unfounded, as a rather drunken and confused Miles called out, 'Help, police!' before being informed that they *were* the police and that he was under arrest.

On Sunday 9 November, at Cannon Row police station, Superintendent Julian cautioned Miles and told him that he was making enquiries regarding the discovery of his parents' bodies on the beach. He broke down, saying, 'I know what you are referring to. I wish to admit everything to you with as little trouble as possible.' He said he did not want Gabrielle brought into the matter, and after being cautioned, told them, 'I had a brainstorm', as if to imply that the killings were not premeditated. He was then formally charged with the murder of his father, aged fifty-three, and his mother, aged fifty-six.

The next day he was taken back to Cornwall. Wearing a fawn check suit and tartan tie, looking tired and his hair dishevelled, he was charged a second time, in the magistrates' court where his father had been Clerk to the Justices for twenty-three years, and was remanded in custody for a further period. The only words he spoke throughout the short hearing were the question, 'May I apply for legal aid?' His uncle, General Sir George Giffard, stepped in and offered to assist him in his defence, and Mr W.G. Scown of St Austell, a well-known advocate in the county who had known Miles for several years, agreed to act on his behalf. The Bodmin District Coroner, Mr E.W. Gill, opened an inquest on the deceased couple and adjourned it indefinitely after hearing evidence of identification given by another of Charles's brothers, Campbell Walter Giffard, a stockbroker, of Melina Place, London.

Charlie Giffard's car, photographed by police shortly after the murders. (© Devon & Cornwall Constabulary)

Miles told the police about the iron pipe which he had thrown into the river at Fenny Bridges. As it had been lying in running water for several days by the time they found it and there were no hairs or blood left on it, but inside there was a residue of mud which matched that on pipes in the garden at Carrickowl and, more significantly, on the car which Charles Giffard had been getting out of when he was attacked.

Though the community around St Austell was shocked by the Giffards' murders, not everybody regretted that Charles had gone, much as they might deplore the manner of his death. One man rang a member of the legal profession to tell him that the solicitor was dead, to which the second man's reaction was 'About time too.' Even some members of the police force thought likewise. When PC Mutton told the Assistant Chief Constable, Reggie Rowland, that Mr Giffard Senior had been murdered, the reply was a succinct 'Serves the bugger right.'

A memorial service was held in the local parish church where they had worshipped for so many years, with two of Charles Giffard's brothers leading the mourners. Robin Giffard, who was in Kenya working on his uncle's farm, was informed of the grim news by telegram but could not return in time.

On 12 December Miles appeared on remand in custody at the court again and was committed for trial at Bodmin Assizes in February 1953. Dr Hocking, the Cornwall county pathologist, had examined the bodies on the beach and said that in both cases injuries had been caused before and after death. Mr Giffard was dead when he was thrown over the cliff. His face had been struck four times and

The body of Charles Giffard. (© Devon & Cornwall Constabulary)

split raggedly open, with another blow on the right collar bone, one or more on the top of his head causing severe bruising, and he had two black eyes. There was further bruising on the back of the right hand extending some six inches up the arm, and marked swelling but no laceration, suggesting that there had been heavy blows on the arm as well as a result of him holding it up to ward off blows aimed at his head.

Both of Mrs Giffard's wrists were broken, probably as a result of her falling on her hands while still conscious, and her lower left arm was broken. There was a deep jagged cut above the eye and both eyes were black, her skull was shattered and the base fractured. Nearly all those injuries must have been caused before death and the only ones sustained afterwards were some of the tears and splits in the scalp and extensive fractures of the skull. She had been beaten around the head at least twice. After this evidence had been presented to the court, the charge was again read to Miles Giffard by the Clerk, and the Chairman formally committed him for trial. His counsel declared that he would plead not guilty to murder, would not call any evidence at that stage, and that one of the defences at the trial would be that he was insane at the time of the killings.

The trial opened on 4 February and lasted for three days. Though Miles' mental state of mind was open to question, the same could not be said about his intention to commit murder. Gabrielle Vallance was one of the first witnesses to be called. She produced the damning letter from him, read out to the court by Mr Scott Henderson, QC for the prosecution, saying that Miles Giffard saw no

Gabriel Vallance outside Bodmin Assizes Court, February 1953. (Ellis Collection, Cornish Studies Library, Redruth)

future, 'short of doing him in'. The killing of his father was not the impulsive action of a hot-tempered young man who had lashed out in a fit of temper, but a clearly premeditated deed. Whether he was intent on the cold-blooded murder of his mother as well was another matter. Dr Craig, who had since left Devon and moved to County Kerry, gave evidence as to his mental condition. George Alexander Keay, Miles's former housemaster at Rugby, and Peter Saunders, a contemporary of Giffard at Blundell's and now studying architecture in London, both testified as to his strange behaviour at school, saying 'he was not at all like other boys'.

On the second day Dr Craig was asked about a letter he had written about Miles in August 1941 to Dr John Hamilton Hood of Truro, the family's General Practitioner. He had warned the latter that 'The door which was closed is slowly opening towards the outside world. We have got to go on if we are to save him from breaking down mentally as he reaches adolescence.' Giffard, Craig maintained, had never fully recovered. Only the disciplined and controlled nature of his life in the Navy enabled him to survive as long as he did. Less sympathetic by nature than Dr Craig, Dr Hood had had more than enough of his young patient. He had never known Charles Giffard to suffer mental disturbances, but he thought the son was 'an idle little waster'. Somewhat startled by this hostile view, Dr Craig hastily said that in his profession he could not possibly subscribe to that word 'waster'. The two men would not agree. Dr Hood had known the family for over twenty years and he said there was nothing wrong with Miles' mental state. The young man, he insisted, was idle, selfish and cared for nothing but his dreams of a sporting career.

A Harley Street psychiatrist, Dr Arthur Picton Rossiter Lewis, said in evidence that he had seen Giffard in prison three times. It was his professional opinion that when Giffard killed his parents he was suffering from a defect of reason due to disease of the mind, but at the time he knew what he was doing to some extent. He did not know that what he was doing was wrong either in the moral sense or in the sense of being against the law, as the disease from which he suffered was a particular form of schizophrenia. The low sugar content of his blood showed he had a defect in his blood of the normal amount of sugar. A person was dependent on his sugar content for efficient working of the brain, and brain cells might not function properly because of the sugar drop. Miles Giffard, said Dr Lewis, was a case in point. Some of the symptoms of his disease would be confusion, irritability, sudden impulsive outbursts, impaired judgment and an inability to distinguish between right and wrong.

When Mr Justice Oliver asked whether these symptoms were commensurate with those of schizophrenia, the psychiatrist affirmed that they were identical. The other doctor who had given evidence, said the judge, had no doubt the prisoner's behaviour was caused by schizophrenia, and did Dr Lewis have any doubt that it was caused by low blood sugar? 'I do not exclude schizophrenia,' was the reply, 'but I think there was a clear explanation for the schizophrenic outburst.'

For the prosecution, Mr Henderson asked whether the psychiatrist was prepared to say that Giffard was suffering from schizophrenia from what he knew of the events of 7 November and what he had seen of the patient? 'No, I should not be able to say that unless I had the earlier history.'

Dr John Matheson, the principal medical officer of Brixton Prison, told the court that an encephalographic examination had been carried out on Giffard during his time in custody, to indicate whether his brain was functioning normally or not. No abnormality was indicated. When questioned about the tests at Wormwood Scrubs into the sugar content of Giffard's blood, Dr Matheson said that Giffard had been deprived of food for twenty-one hours to see whether his sugar content would fall below the danger level.

'But what is the use of getting him below the safety line by starving him?' asked the judge. 'He was not starving on 7 November, was he?' Dr Matheson stated that he was not starving, 'but this is what the authorities lay down as being the way to make this test.' From all that he knew about the events on the night of the killings, he said he failed to find any evidence that Giffard might have been suffering from spontaneous hypoglycaemia. It would be most unlikely for an attack of that kind to occur that evening in view of his hearty lunch that day, and as during the afternoon he had drunk half a bottle of whisky.

The judge had one more question. Referring to the fact that Giffard had moved two very heavy bodies over several hundred yards of very rough ground, had then set to work cleaning up the house, and then driven well over 200 miles to central London – 'you do not think a hypoglycaemic patient could have done that?' 'I am certain he could not,' replied Dr Matheson. From what he knew of Giffard's history before the killings, everything suggested that he did not suffer from mental disease. He would not expect a schizophrenic to drink or to make friends easily, and he did not think Giffard was suffering from schizophrenia that night.

On 6 February, the third and last day of the trial, Matheson was questioned further by John Maude, QC counsel for the defence, about the prisoner's mental condition. He said that 'night terrors' as a child might be significant, but children tended to react out of all proportion to such trivial things, and mental cases were difficult to diagnose. While Giffard might have had hallucinations as a child, and while some of the things he did were peculiar, these could not be taken as proof of mental disease. Giffard had tried to avoid full responsibility for killing his parents, with a statement, 'God knows for what reason I hit them over the head with a piece of iron pipe. I hit him once then he slumped to the ground unconscious. Mother had gone into the house. I went into the house after her. I found her in the kitchen. I hit her from behind. Everything went peculiar. I got into a panic.'

Maude's final questions were very much to the point. Did it not look irrational for the prisoner to murder his mother and father 'in order to go up to see that girl?' When taking into consideration that 'he had been a liar, drinking, stealing from his parents, and so on, there is no doubt that to have killed his parents to go and see this girl is extraordinary?' Matheson agreed that it was, but one of the reasons that he did not think Giffard was going through a 'schizophrenic episode' when he killed his parents was the fact that everything appeared to have been carefully planned. Did he think the plan involved murder, asked Maude. 'It is very hard to say. The only indication is his remark in the letter to the girl – "short of doing him in, I see no future in the world at all."' Such a remark, Matheson went on, could possibly be intended in a jocular way, though the jury must have felt instinctively that in view of events, Giffard was definitely not joking.

Throughout the proceedings, Miles Giffard remained impassive. The only time he showed any sign of emotion was when his mother's death was described, with reference to her being unconscious but still alive when thrown over the cliff.

In summing up, Mr Justice Oliver stated that 'the man who butchered that old man and old lady, if he is not protected by being insane in law, is a murderer.' It was up to the jury to decide whether Giffard knew what he was doing at the time, as the defence did not pretend he did not; and whether at the time he did those acts, did he know he was breaking the law. It was up to the defence to make it at least more likely than not that at the time he did the act he was accused of, he was suffering from some defect of reason, due to some disease of the mind that made it impossible for him to know that what he did was unlawful. He had disturbed his girlfriend in her London house early in the morning, but instead of spending the morning with her, went off with his mother's jewels which he had stolen over her dead body and sold them for £50. Was that the act of a madman, or of somebody who was utterly wicked? As for the blood-sugar tests in prison, he pointed out that the findings applied to a man who had been starved for 26 hours. Could they be compared with those of a man who had just enjoyed a heavy lunch, followed by half a bottle of whisky?

At this stage of the summing-up Mr C.E. Venning, the Under-Sheriff of Cornwall, sitting on the judge's bench, collapsed with a loud cry and had to be

Mr Justice Oliver with policemen and various officials outside Bodmin Court at the time of Miles Giffard's trial. (Ellis Collection, Cornish Studies Library, Redruth)

carried from the court. Resuming, the judge said there could be no acquittal. The prisoner was either mad or bad, guilty or guilty but insane. If he deliberately disposed of his parents' bodies over the cliffs and hoped the sea would wash them away, or if he pushed them over, expecting that the injuries he had inflicted on them would be completely submerged in the wreck that would normally take place involving bodies falling on to rocks 120ft below, in the jury's view did that indicate that he knew he had done wrong when he did that?

The jury retired at 3.32 p.m. and took thirty-five minutes to return a guilty verdict. The judge pronounced sentence of death and later that afternoon Miles was driven to Horfield Prison, Bristol, pending an appeal.

Miles' uncle General Sir George Giffard, who had been Commander-in-Chief in West Africa during the war and had been living in Winchester at the time of the trial, financed his defence and appeal. On 22 February Messrs Stephens & Scown, the St Austell solicitors acting on the prisoner's behalf, stated that a member of the jury which had tried him had written to the Home Secretary that he was convinced Giffard was insane when he killed his parents. The juror added that because of a misunderstanding, Mr Justice Oliver had not been informed. Mr Scown said a letter had been sent to the Home Secretary eleven days earlier informing him thus. A reply was subsequently received from the Home Office saying that the juror in question had already written directly to the Home Secretary, who had considered all aspects of the case before arriving at his decision not to grant a reprieve. When asked about a suggestion that the verdict of the jury would appear not to have been unanimous, the spokesman replied, 'That point goes to the secrecy of the jury room, and we cannot comment upon it.'

Other submissions were made to the Home Secretary from members of the public and from the headmaster at Blundell's among others, all bearing witness to his disturbed state of mind. The appeal was dismissed and on 24 February Miles Giffard was hanged at Horfield.

A few days later General Giffard wrote a letter to *The Times*, published on 7 March. It drew attention to his nephew's long history of abnormality and mental illness from the age of four, the fact that a specialist examined him when he was aged fifteen, and that his parents were warned of the possibility of mental breakdown in the future. After he left the Royal Navy he began once again to show symptoms of mental illness; but his father was ill at the time, no treatment was administered and it culminated in the grim events of November 1952. 'It is impossible for any ordinary human being to know how the mind of another is working,' he concluded, 'and for a jury to be expected to decide on February 6 how the mind of a man suffering from mental illness was working on the night of November 7 seems to the ordinary layman absurd. To decide such cases by rules which in the light of present-day knowledge are admitted to be in need of revision seems to me to be manifestly unjust.'

Nevertheless most of the jury, and many of those in the local community, were not convinced by the arguments as to Miles Giffard's lack of sanity. Charles Giffard had not been a likeable man or an admirable father, but the evidence that his son had put in writing that he planned to 'do the old man in' a few days beforehand, and had then set about killing his mother with equal violence, forfeited the young man of most if not all of any sympathy which might have been felt for him.

24

DEATH OF A RECLUSE

Constantine, 1963

William Garfield Rowe was born in 1899, the son of parents who lived and farmed near Porthleven. They were staunch pacifists, and in 1917 he was conscripted into the army. Reluctantly leaving Venta Vedna, the family home, he returned within less than a week, vowing he would never have anything to do with the war. His parents and brothers applauded him as a deserter with the courage to uphold his convictions, welcomed him home briefly, gave him £50 and sent him away before the authorities could find him. Relations and neighbours were told that he had returned to his unit, though in fact he had gone into hiding. Before long he was traced by the Military Police, arrested and taken to a detention centre, but escaped and returned home.

In order to avoid being arrested a second time, he remained a total recluse, only venturing out of the house under cover of darkness to help work in the fields. His father and brothers were often seen by neighbours cutting and bundling corn, picking and loading vegetables – but William himself remained virtually invisible to the outside world. Anybody who dared to ask was told that he had never returned home from active service, like so many other young men of his generation. Those who wondered why the family were so punctilious about locking and bolting the doors of their home every time they went out put it down to the eccentricity of a close-knit family who had suffered bereavement. Nobody apparently noticed that his name was absent from the local war memorial.

When the Second World War broke out in 1939, the family became apprehensive again lest any civil servants checking up on them would find out the truth. As a result nobody ever registered him for the purposes of obtaining an identity or ration card, or clothing coupons. The family's farm proved largely self-sufficient in providing the food they needed.

When William's father died in 1949, the family moved to Nanjarrow, an isolated farmhouse near Constantine. Standing at the end of about half a mile of a very rough cart track and one and a half miles from the nearest main road, this five-bedroomed property was ideal for continuing to conceal the identity of the man who to all outside appearances no longer existed. Yet nobody took any chances while they were moving house, and as the procession of carts went from Venta Vedna to Nanjarrow, one contained a pile of sacks, carefully concealing William Rowe.

In 1954 his brother Stanley, who like William had never married, but stayed at home and taken over responsibility for running the farm since their father's

Nanjarrow Farm. (© Devon & Cornwall Constabulary)

death, died. The other brother, Joel, had married and lived with his family nearby. William and his mother split the work on a shift basis, she working by day and he by night, until she died two years later.

Fortunately for him, at the start of Queen Elizabeth II's reign an amnesty had been declared for all who had deserted during both wars. At last, now in his mid-fifties, William could abandon his reclusive lifestyle if he so chose. Though he no longer had to remain indoors during the hours of daylight, needless to say, adjusting to such a change in his life was not easy. The farmhouse was a reasonable size, but he lived in one downstairs room, all the others being stacked from floor to ceiling with furniture and general family possessions accumulated over the years. He continued to look after his cattle and pigs, with the difference that he could now go to market and also to the shops. Any local excitement that may have been caused by his reappearance did not last long. Yet years of living a hermit-like existence had made him very shy and reserved, and he was content to keep his own company. Visitors to the farm were not welcomed, especially not his brother Joel, with whom he was never on good terms. When cattle dealers called, he would always carry on any conversation in a farmyard or outbuilding, rather than invite them into the house.

However, less savoury elements in the neighbourhood decided that any recluse was bound to be wealthy. While Rowe was out shopping one day in 1960 an intruder broke in, stealing at least £200 in cash and some of his late mother's trinkets.

The dining room at Nanjarrow Farm. (© Devon & Cornwall Constabulary)

Far worse was to happen three years later. On 14 August 1963, at about 9.15 p.m., he was noticed by a neighbour completing his farmyard jobs for the day, then locking and bolting his doors as usual. Next morning PC James received an urgent call from a neighbour to say a dead body had been seen on the premises at Nanjarrow. James, several other officers and Dr Hocking called to investigate and found William Rowe covered in blood, lying huddled face downwards with one arm outstretched in a corner of the farmyard. Bloodstains led to the farmhouse door, with a pool of blood by the doorstep and splashes on the door framework. There were drag marks in the mud between the door and the body, and mud had been heaped up under the man's face. Temperature recordings suggested that the time of death had been late on 14 August, between 10 p.m. and midnight. The house had been ransacked, with cupboards thrown open, furniture overturned and clothing strewn around at random.

A post-mortem examination revealed numerous injuries, some stab wounds inflicted with a dagger or similar weapon, and other blows from a blunt instrument. There were five stab wounds in the chest, one of which had penetrated the heart, two the upper surface of the liver. Another wound ran horizontally in the upper part of the neck on the right side, penetrating as far back as the spine, severing the main blood vessels on the side of the neck, and another, more superficial cut on the front of the neck. The head had been battered by several blows, with six ragged splits in the scalp. Both eyes were blackened.

There were also scrapes, abrasions and cuts on the front of the face, and a ragged cut two inches long along the line of the lower jaw, the bone of which was shattered. These injuries had probably been caused by the body falling forwards on to the hard courtyard and then being dragged into the corner where it was found. The skull was shattered, with portions of bone depressed inwards, and the brain was bruised and lacerated.

Rowe had tried to defend himself from the attacks. The top of the third finger on his left hand was severed through the last joint. There were four heavy blows on the right arm, in a position to suggest that he had raised his arm to shield his head. Where the blows had fallen, the skin was split and a large bruise over the whole of the back of the left hand was further indication of his efforts to protect himself. Death was due to a combined attack made simultaneously by two assailants, one with a knife or dagger, the other with a blunt instrument.

Murder headquarters were set up in a nearby school, with a team including Cornwall Constabulary detectives Superintendent Tommy Walke, Superintendent Richard Dunn, Detective Inspector Bob Eden and Detective Sergeant Norman Arscott. Chief Constable Richard Matthews telephoned Scotland Yard for assistance and by that evening Detective Superintendent Maurice Osborn and Detective Sergeant Andrew McPhee had come from London to assist.

Meanwhile five people were living at Kenwyn Hill caravan site, on the outskirts of Truro. The site, with about seventy vans, was owned by Charles Penhaligon, a well-respected businessman in the area and inspector in the local constabulary. Among those who lived here were newly married couples awaiting a council house, some who had just obtained work in Truro and were house-hunting,

Dennis John Whitty. (© Cornish Photonews Ltd)

and various casual labourers who tended not to stay long but were liable to give the place a bad name. Living in one such caravan were three girls, all aged nineteen, and two male labourers. Russell Pascoe, a married man of twenty-three from Constantine who had recently left his wife, made a living by doing odd jobs in the area, while Dennis John Whitty, one year younger and engaged, was employed at Truro gas works. On 14 August Pascoe had asked one of the girls, Norma Booker, for some nylon stockings as they wanted to 'do a job'. Notwithstanding any suspicions she may have had about their motives, Booker handed a pair over. Pascoe was not a man to whom one said no lightly.

That evening the men set off on Pascoe's motorcycle without saying anything more. They took a starting pistol, iron bar and knife with them. When they returned to the caravan in the small hours of 15 August, according to the girls, Whitty was grinning, while Pascoe looked ill at ease and was seen wiping blood from Whitty's face. Whitty said there had been an incident involving a farmer, while Pascoe muttered, 'We didn't get nothin'.' The girls were told not to breathe a word about their absence and the men went to their usual jobs that morning.

Later that day, Pascoe's girlfriend bought a local evening paper and showed Whitty the story giving details of the discovery of Rowe's body. 'You went to Constantine,' she told him. 'Did you do this?' Whitty admitted that he had. At this point Pascoe came into the caravan kitchen and said that if the girls opened their mouths they would end up the same way as the farmer. One of the men said there had been trouble and Mr Rowe had been killed because he recognised them.

Russell Pascoe. (© Cornish Photonews Ltd)

The girls themselves were no saints. They had not uttered a word of protest when Pascoe and Whitty had said they were going to 'do a job', though they knew what was meant. There may have been an element of self-preservation in this, but they had been willing partners in crime before. Two of them had accompanied the men on shop and housebreaking forays, and at least once one of the girls had carried an iron bar herself, ready to hit a night porter should one be in the way when they went to burgle a public house.

As part of the police investigation, roadblocks had been set up around the area. On 16 August Detective Sergeant Arscott saw Pascoe riding his motorcycle in Constantine. The police had had their suspicions about him for some time, so Arscott stopped him and asked him to go to the murder headquarters for routine questioning. Pascoe duly did so, and told Detective Superintendent Osborn that he had read about the murder in the paper. When asked about his movements at the time, he said he had been at the caravan with Whitty and the three girls that night. When asked if he knew Mr Rowe of Nanjarrow Farm, Pascoe replied that he had known him for some time and worked for him 'three or four years ago.' That would have been about the time that the farm was robbed in Rowe's absence.

Pascoe and Whitty were known to be acquainted with each other and the police decided to call the latter for questioning as well. On 17 August Pascoe was taken into the charge room at Falmouth police station, and Osborn told him that he had 'good reason to believe that you and Dennis Whitty killed Mr Rowe.' After being given the usual caution, Pascoe gave a statement in which he said he only knocked Rowe over the head with a bar. 'I told Dennis that was enough, but he went mad with the knife. I will tell you the truth. Last Wednesday night with my mate, Dennis Whitty, I went to Mr Rowe's farm. We went on my motorbike. We were going to see if he had any money. We knocked on the door about eleven o'clock. The old man answered the door. Dennis was standing in front of the door. He said he was a helicopter pilot and had crashed. I hit the old man at the back of the head with a small iron bar. I meant to knock him out, that's all. He [Whitty] took the iron bar and went for him. I had to walk away, honest I did. I went inside and found £4 under a piano. Denis took a watch and two big boxes of matches and some keys from the old man's pockets. We shared £4 – £2 each. I have spent mine.'

Pascoe continued to deny to Osborn that he had killed Rowe. Whitty, he said, 'went mad', and he was afraid to stop him 'or he would stick me. I had to walk away. I couldn't stop him. He said he finished him when he stuck the knife in his throat. I only knocked him over the head with a bar. I just knocked him out. When I did, I told Dennis that was enough, but he went mad with the knife. Then he kept the bar from me and kept thumping him on the head.'

Both assailants seemed determined to blame the other for Rowe's violent death. When the police told Whitty that he and Pascoe were both responsible, he was adamant that 'Pascoe made me stick him.' When charged and cautioned, he seemed to accept the inevitability of their fate. 'We are both over twenty-one, so I suppose we can hang?' The police told him that it was not for them to decide, but if convicted of the offence with which they were charged, they could face execution.

Whitty then realised that there was no point in trying to evade the consequences of their actions any longer. 'I want to tell you about it. I was going to give myself up if I hadn't been brought in.' Under caution, he made a written statement confirming that it had been at the suggestion of Pascoe that they went to Nanjarrow for money. 'I didn't want to go, but he made me. I knocked and the old man came to the door with a lantern. I told him I'd had trouble with a helicopter and asked the old man to show me the phone.' At the time he had been wearing dark jeans and a dark double-breasted blazer with silver buttons which in poor light could have been taken for naval uniform.

Continuing his statement, Whitty said that Pascoe, who had been hiding against the wall, then hit Rowe on the head with an iron bar. The old man fell down and Pascoe kept hitting him, at the same time telling Whitty to 'stick him'. 'I didn't want to and I started crying. He told me he would use the bar on me if I didn't do it, so I stuck him in the chest three or four times and once in the throat, I think.' Pascoe then made him drag the body to a corner of the yard and take some keys from the pocket, they went in the house and took two packets of matches and an old watch. He had no idea what Pascoe did with the keys, but he threw the knife away and dropped the bar in the dam.

In his statement, Pascoe said that on their way back to the caravan they threw the bar and the knife in the Argel Dam reservoir. The police later recovered both weapons. One was an iron jemmy, about 14ins long, weighing 2lb and 5oz. The other was a sheath knife, 6ins long, sharpened on both sides, tapering to a point.

Pascoe and Whitty were jointly charged at Penryn Magistrates' Court on 19 August, remanded in custody, and appeared at court again on 26 September for the preliminary hearing of the Crown's case against them. The extent of Rowe's injuries as revealed by the prosecution horrified everyone present in court. John Woods, Director of Public Prosecutions, said that the obvious motive for this murder was theft, 'and this was murder in the furtherance of theft. Never has the well-worn phrase 'savage and brutal attack' been more typified than by this case.' In the space of about thirty seconds, he went on, the victim had sustained injuries including six or seven ragged cuts in his scalp, a shattered skull, a fractured jaw, and five chest wounds including one five inches deep inflicted by a stiletto-type knife which had penetrated the heart. Part of one finger of the right hand had been completely severed, an indication of how hard he had struggled to defend himself against his attackers.

The murder, Woods concluded, was premeditated to the extent that both men had agreed they were going out in the furtherance of theft. They had every intention of hitting anybody they encountered, as typified by the helicopter story; it was a cold-blooded and ruthless murder committed in the furtherance of gain and greed.

The trial of Pascoe and Whitty opened at Bodmin Assizes on 29 October 1963. A jury of nine men and three women heard Norman Skelhorn, QC counsel for Whitty's defence, enter a plea of 'not guilty', and James Comyn make a similar plea on behalf of Pascoe. According to Dr Hocking, Whitty may have been short of stature and the younger of the two, but he was 'almost a little weasel of a man' and it soon became apparent that he was the dominant partner in crime, whereas Pascoe was 'a simple lad, easily led'.

On the first day, Osborn brought forward new evidence when he revealed that the police suspected a sum amounting to thousands of pounds remained hidden in the fields and cowsheds at Nanjarrow, although a thorough two-day search by the police had initially brought very little of it to light. About £20 in silver had been found concealed in jam jars, a milk churn and among old clothes. Further investigations on the premises revealed a tattered two-page document in Rowe's handwriting, which proved to be the key to a buried sum of £3,000 in £5 notes. The paper had been written in Spanish, with the aid of a copy of *Teach Yourself Spanish*, and contained several clues which led the police to the discovery of large sums of money hidden all over the farm. Only then did they realise that Rowe had spent much of his daylight hours, while concealed in the house, studying in order to better himself.

Comyn described the case as 'one of the most horrible and gruesome murders ever known in this county or in this country'. He appealed to the jury not to let horror blind them to the need for care in reaching a verdict, and warned them against being carried away by feelings of wrath or indignation. The nature of the evidence, he said, should be considered with extra caution. Pascoe, he went on, had 'a discreditable story to tell, but there was never one single instance when he was trapped. It is my submission that he told his story well and told it truthfully.'

On behalf of Whitty, Skelhorn suggested that either he was acting under the influence, fear and pressure of the suggestion of the more forceful Pascoe; or that his psychiatric background was such as to make him guilty of the lesser charge of manslaughter on the grounds of diminished responsibility. It was Pascoe's idea, he submitted, that they should carry out the robbery on Rowe's farm, especially as Pascoe had admitted to the theft at Nanjarrow a few years earlier. Skelhorn reminded the jury of Whitty's claim that when he had told Pascoe he did not want to be involved, Pascoe had threatened him; 'You will have to come. If you don't, I will scar you for life.'

Whitty's mental state was clearly an issue. Skelhorn said that he suffered from hysteria and a tendency to have blackouts. Pascoe's claims that Whitty 'went mad with the knife', he declared, were consistent with the action of a man not totally in control of himself. Giving evidence on his own behalf, Whitty spoke of 'strange and unnatural things' that he claimed had happened to him, among them watching doors opening themselves for no good reason and pictures changing overnight. He said he believed in ghosts, and early one day at 4 a.m. he saw a figure with wings in the sky as he was walking down to the beach.

One witness called for the defence was David Penhaligon, the nineteen-year-old son of the owner of Kenwyn Hill caravan site. He told the court that on one occasion, while at the family bungalow, he had been asked for help by some passers-by who had found a man they thought had been knocked down by a car. At once Penhaligon recognised the man as Dennis Whitty. He seemed to be unconscious, with bruises and scratches on his face, so they called an ambulance and took him to hospital. Some days later Whitty called at the bungalow and thanked Penhaligon for his help, explaining that he had not been knocked down, but had just had an epileptic fit. This added to Whitty's defence that he became uncontrollably violent when attacked by epilepsy, and that he had had such a fit while robbing Rowe.

Although Penhaligon's parents had both been staunch Conservatives, his experiences as a witness inspired him to join the Liberal Party, as he was profoundly shocked that the court 'showed no understanding of what it was like to live on the fringes of society'. Living alongside some of the poorest people in the Truro area, he had seen the day-to-day difficulties faced by less fortunate members of the community, problems that could not be solved by what he called the typical middle-class response of 'they should pull themselves together'. In December 1974, a few weeks after his election as Liberal Member of Parliament for Truro, in a Commons debate he voted against restoration of the death penalty. Nevertheless, after another similar debate one year later he supported a motion calling for further investigation into whether or not it should be reintroduced for acts of terrorism that caused death.

Shortly before his untimely death in a car accident in December 1986, Penhaligon recalled the trial in a radio programme. He said that his evidence in the court at Bodmin was followed by that of three psychiatrists, who were asked whether Whitty had acted under the influence of hysteria. The first one took an hour to say he did not know; the second took three quarters of an hour to say 'he could have done'. The third took four minutes to tell the court, 'Garn, he's having you on' – and he was the only one to be believed. The member for Truro wondered whether if he had given the same evidence as David Penhaligon, forty-two-year-old MP and chartered engineer, as opposed to David Penhaligon, nineteen-year-old fitter-and-turner apprentice, his testimony would have made more of an impression.

On the final day of the trial, 2 November, the judge, Mr Justice Thesiger, told the jury that he would ask them to say whether or not it was their opinion that Whitty was acting under fear of grievous bodily harm, or even death, from the ruthless Pascoe. Regarding Skelhorn's second defence, that of diminished responsibility, the judge asserted that mental responsibility depended on a man's ability to know what he was doing and that he would be punished if he was caught. The jury had to decide whether there was any abnormality in Whitty's mind and if there was evidence of hysterical behaviour. He thought it significant that the prisoner's 'hysterical attacks' were manifested in blackouts and moments of unconsciousness. The result of his attacks of mental abnormality, he said, were the fits of unconsciousness. There was no evidence that he had suffered a fit or blackout on the night of the murder.

In his final speech for the prosecution, Norman Brodrick QC asked the jury to accept that Whitty used a knife to stab Mr Rowe while Pascoe struck him with an iron bar. Skelhorn submitted that Whitty did what he was forced to do under threats from Pascoe, that he suffered from mental hysteria and could claim diminished responsibility. He asked for an acquittal on the murder charge and a verdict of manslaughter. Comyn likewise urged the jury not to find his client Pascoe guilty of murder. The jury took four and a half hours before they returned to record verdicts of guilty against both prisoners. Mr Justice Thesiger said he 'entirely agreed' with them; 'I think they were the only possible verdicts in this case.'

After sentence of death had been pronounced, the condemned men were driven away from the Assize Court. Three weeks later their appeals were heard and rejected by the Court of Appeal. Their executions were set for 17 December; Pascoe at Horfield Prison, Bristol, and Whitty at Winchester.

In Falmouth a petition was started, not so much for the reprieve of both men as for the abolition of capital punishment, but less than 600 people signed. One of the disappointed organisers commented that the response seemed to be in favour of the hangman; 'this appeared to be out of an emotion born of revenge and not from a desire for punishment.' Those who had been arguing and campaigning throughout the country for the abolition of the death penalty had undoubtedly underestimated the sheer revulsion felt by most people in the community at such a barbaric crime. The two young men who were prepared to rob a defenceless elderly man and commit such a callous murder in the process plainly deserved what was coming to them.

On 13 December Rowe's provisional will was published, which gave the value of his property, goods and chattels as £8,082. It was assumed that most of this related to Nanjarrow, but an element of it included the cash recovered. Meanwhile Rowe's brother had taken over the running of Nanjarrow, and in order to discourage sightseers he surrounded the property with barbed wire barricades and 'Keep Out' notices.

Pascoe celebrated his twenty-fourth birthday in Horfield. On the evening of 16 December, he was visited in his cell by the Bishop of Bristol, Dr Tomkins. At Pascoe's request the Bishop baptized and confirmed him, and offered him Holy Communion. That same evening Bridget Hamilton, Whitty's nineteen-year-old fiancée, was allowed into the prison at Winchester to say farewell to him. Earlier that day she had stood weeping on the steps of the Home Office in London as members of the 'Committee of 100', a group which had set up to organise mass sit-ins and blockades, attempted to stage a peaceful demonstration there. They also handed in a petition, signed by over 2,000, asking the Home Secretary, Henry Brooke, to advise the Queen to exercise her prerogative of mercy. Later they tried to see him at the House of Commons, but without success. All-night vigils by anti-capital punishment demonstrators were held outside Brooke's home in his London constituency of Hampstead, as well as outside both prisons. Among the protesters at Horfield was Tony Benn, Labour Member of Parliament for Bristol South-East.

On the morning of 17 December both men were hanged. Within the next few months there would be only one more murder case on mainland Britain, again a robbery in which the victim was killed in cold blood by two perpetrators, which would lead to the gallows. One year after Pascoe and Whitty paid with their lives, campaigners for the abolition of the death penalty for murder had their way with the first reading of the Murder (Abolition of the Death Penalty) Bill, and Royal Assent was given to the Act in November 1965, suspending capital punishment for murder for five years. In December 1969 a further parliamentary vote reaffirmed the decision that it should be permanently abolished.

BIBLIOGRAPHY & REFERENCES

Where individual newspapers or journal articles have been consulted for specific cases, these are cited in the list below. Most of the books that follow have been consulted in the research for several chapters. Certain websites have also been used, but are not listed as they are liable to disappear suddenly from the internet.

NEWSPAPER AND JOURNAL REFERENCES

3. 'Should you like to go to heaven, dear?' 1824
The Times, 6 April 1824

4. Fizzy Maggy, 1836
The West Briton, 26 February 1836, 1 and 8 April 1836

5. 'Come, I suppose she has found the Lord now', 1839
The West Briton, February and March 1839 (internet transcripts)

6. 'Do, Willy, go and confess', 1840
The Times, 28 February 1840, 2 and 20 April 1840; *The West Briton* 18, 21 and 28 February 1840; 13 and 27 March 1840; 3 and 17 April 1840

7. 'See, what a wretched end I have come to', 1844
The Times, 1 and 10 May 1844

8. 'Hold your noise, or I will give you a slap', 1878
The Times, 29 July 1878, 16 August 1878; *Western Morning News,* 29 July 1878

9. 'It is well taken care of', 1882
The Times, 31 July and 28 October 1882; *Western Morning News,* 10 and 31 July, 28 October 1882

10. 'I will soon settle the lot of you', 1886
The Times, 30 July 1886; *Western Morning News,* 30 July 1886

11. Murder in Falmouth Harbour, 1886, 1887 and 1901
The Times, **18.4.1901;** *West Briton,* 22 August 1887, 29 September 1887; *Western Morning News,* 18 June 1901

12. 'I suppose it was temper', 1909
Western Morning News, 4 May and 25 June 1909

13. 'I believe I have done it', 1910
The Times, 18 August 1910 and 22 October 1910; *Western Morning News*, 18 August 1910 and 22 October 1910

14. 'All that a man could wish for', 1920
The Times, 27 and 28 January 1920, 13 February 1920

15. 'Never had poison of any kind', 1921
The Times, 15, 16, 17, 18, 22, 23 November 1921, 19 December 1921, 2 and 23 January 1922, 3 February 1922, 7 March 1922; *Western Morning News*, 15, 16, 17, 18, 19, 21, 22, 24 November 1921, 2 and 23 January 1922, 2 and 3 February 1922

16. 'They had very serious trouble', 1923
The Cornish and Devon Post (Launceston edition), 28 April 1923

17. 'Be a trump, take and do it', 1928
The Post (Launceston Edition), 25 February 1928, 3, 10 and 17 March 1928, 21 April 1928, 1 June 1928, 17 and 28 July 1928

18. 'They will blame one of us', 1930
Marshall, Walter, 'The Bude Enigma Reinvestigated', *True Detective*, November 1997; *The Post* (Launceston edition), 28 February 1931, 7, 14 and 21 March, 20 and 27 June 1931

19. 'I did not do it wilfully', 1931
The Times, 25 June 1931; *The Post*, 28 February and 27 June 1931

20. 'They are gone away for good', 1937
The Times, 30 April, 2 and 3 June, 13 July 1937; *Western Morning News,* 1 May, 2 and 16 June 1937

21. Murder on Christmas Eve, 1942
Western Morning News, 28 and 29 December 1942, 12, 13, 15, 16 February 1943

22. 'Please, don't let us think of Saturday', 1943
The Times, 17 November, 15 December 1943, 22 January 1944

23. 'I have had a terrible row with the old man', 1952
The Blundellian, July 1943; *The Times* 10, 11 and 20 November 1952, 5, 6, 7, 23 and 25 February 1953, 7 March 1953; *Western Morning News*, 5 February 1953

24. Death of a recluse, 1963
The Times, 20 August, 27 September, 31 October, 4 November, 17 and 18 December 1963

OFFICIAL DOCUMENTS

Cornwall Records Office CRO X 106/36

BOOKS

Bird, Sheila, *Cornish Tales of Mystery and Murder*, Newbury, Countryside, 2002
Eddleston, John J., *The Encyclopedia of Executions*, London, John Blake, 2004
Fielding, Steve, *The Hangman's Record, Vol. 1, 1868–1899; Vol. 2, 1900–1929; Vol. 3, 1930–1964*, Beckenham, CBD, 1994–2005
Hocking, Dr Denis, *Bodies and Crimes: A Pathologist's Casebook*, Brighton, Book Guild, 1992; London, Arrow, 1994
Johnson, Bill, *History of Bodmin Gaol*, Bodmin Town Museum, 2006
Oxford Dictionary of National Biography
Penhaligon, Annette, *Penhaligon*, London, Bloomsbury, 1989
Wilson, Colin, introduced by, *Murder in the Westcountry*, Bodmin, Bossiney, 1975
Wynn, Douglas, *On Trial for Murder*, London, Pan, 2003

TELEVISION

'Roy Marsden's Casebook: Mouse or Monster?' (Documentary on Edward and Annie Black), Prospero/Eagle Media for ITV, broadcast 29 March 2007

INDEX